GREATEST
MOMENTS
IN
BYU
SPORTS

GREATEST MOMENTS
IN
BYU SPORTS

Brad Rock · Lee Warnick

Bookcraft
Salt Lake City, Utah

To Julie and Lori

Library of Congress Catalog Card Number: 84-71985
ISBN 0-88494-536-7

First Printing, 1984

Lithographed in the United States of America
PUBLISHERS PRESS
Salt Lake City, Utah

Contents

Acknowledgments

The chapters in this book describe great athletic moments occurring through outstanding teamwork. We have been the beneficiaries of the same sort of teamwork in putting the book together.

First, our thanks to Dave Schulthess, Ralph Zobell, and Louise Fausett of BYU's Sports Information Office for generously opening their files—and minds—to our research efforts. Their abilities and cooperation are the foundation upon which this book was built.

Brigham Young University photographer Mark Philbrick went the extra mile in sharing visual images of these memorable moments with you. Mel Rogers of KBYU-TV was a patient and thorough guide through miles of sports videotapes. Assistant Athletic Director Pete Witbeck provided valuable background and otherwise hard-to-obtain information.

Though former BYU athletes are spread all over the country, football secretary Shirley Johnson and basketball secretary Linda Feliz always seemed to know where and how to contact them.

And finally, thanks to George Bickerstaff and Andy Allison of Bookcraft for their professionalism and patience throughout the project. They helped make this a "greatest moment" for us.

The Miracle Bowl

A damp winter chill clung to the southern California coast as evening deepened into night at San Diego's Jack Murphy Stadium. It had been mild—in the 60s—at the start of the 1980 Holiday Bowl but now, late in the fourth quarter, temperatures had dropped, fog crouching over the stadium as the field lights slanted down through the thickening mist. Brigham Young University quarterback Jim McMahon checked the scoreboard.

Three seconds.

Wide receiver Dan Plater waited impatiently on the sidelines, hands on hips, as Cougar offensive coordinator Doug Scovil hurriedly gave him the last play to take to the huddle. He put a hand on Plater's shoulder pad. "Save the game pass," he said. "Send Clay [Brown] down the middle; you and Bill [Davis] flank in and look for the tip."

Plater was already moving onto the field. "You want the running backs down?" he called back.

"Yeah."

McMahon reached the sidelines beside head coach LaVell Edwards just as Scovil was talking to Plater. Edwards gave him the same instructions.

Returning to the field McMahon huddled his team, the noise from above washing over the playing field. Despite the bedlam it was strangely quiet in the huddle as McMahon, his voice hoarse and anxious, called the play. Big-time, sophisticated football wasn't what he had in mind. This one was strictly sandlot.

"O.K. Clay, go to the middle. Bill and Danny, go down and loop to the middle. Everybody get in the end zone. I'm throwing it up."

They broke the huddle as the noise continued to build. Plater went wide to one side, Davis to the other, Brown in tight. Knowing the receivers would be unable to hear his signals above the crowd, McMahon had instructed them to go on the first count.

The ball rested on Southern Methodist University's 41-yard line as they set up. The teams hunched for only an instant, the only movement the steam from their breath. The snap came. McMahon dropped back as seven SMU defenders moved toward the end zone.

Just beyond the 50 McMahon, destined to become the top passing quarterback in college football history, planted his feet . . . :02 . . . :01 . . . snapped back his arm . . . :00 . . . and let go . . .

"Save the Game" pass.

All other plays have a number. This one went only by the pretentious title of Save the Game, pure and simple. The play had never been used and never been practiced during the season. Perhaps twice in the 1979 season had they even run through the play in practice. It was like a classic collector's auto from bygone years, to be admired and bragged over— noted for its craftsmanship and beauty but impractical for actual use.

In truth, there hadn't been much reason to resurrect the play during the season. BYU had breezed through an 11-1 year, the only hitch coming in the first game when the highly favored Cougars were upset 25-21 by New Mexico.

From then on it had been a study in superlatives. McMahon had set about establishing himself as the greatest in the line of famous BYU quarterbacks, setting 27 NCAA offensive records and being named to the Kodak all-America team as a junior. Brown also earned all-America status and was often mentioned as the best tight end in the country, a hulking man with sure hands and formidable strength.

The Cougars followed the loss to New Mexico with a rout of San Diego State on regional television. They met a Big 10 opponent for the first time in the school's history and battered Wisconsin 28-3 on a sunny September day in Madison. It was followed by wins over Long Beach State (41-25), Wyoming (52-17), Utah State (70-46), Hawaii (34-7), Texas-El Paso (83-7), North Texas State (41-23), Colorado State (45-14), Utah (56-6) and Nevada-Las Vegas (54-14).

Still, despite the giddy success, the Cougars had endured their share of wrath that season. In the emotional game with Utah State, defensive tackle Pulusila Filiaga had lost his head and struck an official, drawing a suspension for the remainder of the season. BYU's startling point totals and winning margins drew heavy criticism from several news outlets, concerned that Edwards's team was unduly running up the score on weak opponents.

McMahon, too, drew his share of criticism. His

candid response to sensitive questions kept him in the spotlight much of the year. A Catholic, he was asked in every city why he was playing at an LDS school. His answer — because Notre Dame didn't recruit him. One Milwaukee writer quoted McMahon saying he didn't like the pressure they put on him at BYU to conform and that he couldn't wait to get his religion requirements finished. During Holiday Bowl week a Los Angeles paper described how he conducted an interview while dipping snuff.

McMahon's play was nothing short of phenomenal and he drew the resultant national publicity. In the type of performance that becomes legend, he started the game against Hawaii, though only moments before kickoff time he had been expected to sit on the sidelines, due to a shoulder injury the week before. He proceeded to throw an astonishing 60 passes, completing 31. He stunned onlookers on a fourth-down play when, trapped, he swerved past a defensive lineman and punted the ball 33 yards *with his left foot*, forcing Hawaii to take the ball on its own one-yard line.

Indeed, McMahon had become the media's anti-hero; the black sheep superstar amid the fold. One who, whether he chose to or not, carried the dreams of a team and represented a church he didn't belong to.

Bowl week was difficult. BYU was carrying a monkey on its back — despite four appearances it had never won a bowl game. The Cougars had lost in the Fiesta Bowl to Oklahoma State in 1974 and in 1976 dropped a Tangerine Bowl game to the same team. In the inaugural Holiday Bowl the Cougars had botched a 16-3 lead in the third quarter by allowing Navy a 23-16 win.

The next year things got worse. Indiana, a team

the Cougars felt they were superior to, won when BYU kicker Brent Johnson missed a 27-yard field goal with seven seconds left.

Though the players tried to maintain a calm exterior, an air of desperation lingered. Some said they had nothing to prove, knowing all the while they did. The bowl game losing streak was raised in every press conference during the week, prompting Edwards's crack during a civic gathering, "If we don't win a bowl game before I die, I'm afraid my epitaph will read: 'He won a thousand games but couldn't win a bowl game.' "

There was added uneasiness because Scovil, often credited with having developed the wildly successful BYU passing game, had accepted a job as head coach at San Diego State. When asked by a Salt Lake *Tribune* writer if he would miss Scovil the next year McMahon replied, "Sure I will, but remember, I throw the ball. Coach Scovil hasn't completed a pass all year."

As game day neared the anxiety increased when receiver Matt Braga stepped in a hole on the practice field, hyper-extending his knee. It troubled him right up to the opening kickoff and he limped noticeably as he took the field.

While some players took in the charms of the place that calls itself "America's Finest City," others preferred to concentrate almost wholly on the game. The Cougars practiced daily, running and re-running patterns they knew by heart. They worked out under the lights to simulate game conditions.

But not once, ever, did anybody mention using the Save the Game Pass.

The play was designed for only one purpose: to win the game. If it didn't work, all you could say is you lost.

The idea was not necessarily that the tight end

should catch the ball; if the game comes to that desperate stage, everybody on planet Earth knows what is coming, i.e. a bomb pass to the center of the field. As a result, a half dozen or more people from the other team are waiting in the end zone to knock down the throw.

In the Save the Game play, by contrast, the receivers were to drift to the middle while the tight end went after the high throw. Because chances were heavily against his catching the pass, the hope was for a pass interference call to give the offense the ball on the 1-foot line and 25 seconds to run a play (a game can't end on a penalty). Another possibility: the tight end might tip the ball to another receiver. While the options seemed doubtful, the offense wouldn't have much else to choose from.

Still, tight end Clay Brown figured if the ball was coming his direction he had a fair enough chance at catching it. "My role on a lot of plays is to be a decoy," said Brown to a Dallas writer during the week preceding the game. "But SMU better honor me, because if they don't, I'll get the big one."

Jesse Craig James, one of the two best prep running backs in Texas in 1978 — the other being SMU teammate Eric Dickerson — was still catching his breath as he walked off the practice field and up the gradual incline to the stadium dressing rooms a quarter mile away. Though he went by Craig, his father had tagged the Jesse on because he liked the ring.

He spoke in the soft, drawling vernacular of the affluent Houston suburb he hailed from, his politeness in marked contrast to the punishing way he carried the football. There was no outlaw in this Jesse James. He fielded the reporter's questions easily until one, finally, gave him pause.

"A prediction," he smiled. "You really want to know? Well, O.K. I'd say about 21-17. Uh, for SMU."

Thursday night the Cougars met in a conference room at the San Diego Hilton to go over strategy with the various position coaches. As the meeting ended, Mel Farr, the team's 5-foot-2 manager moved to the front of the room as the players gathered around in anticipation. Mel pulled a San Diego phone book from under his arm.

It wasn't the first time he had endeavored to tear a phone book in half purely for the sake of drama. He had begun by tearing apart Hayward, California, phone books and had done the same to the Provo directory several times before big games. This, however, was big city stuff. "Wrist strength and concentration," Mel explained.

He started tearing.

His face reddened, his knuckles whitened. His shoulders trembled slightly. Slowly, the pages began to give. He didn't pay much attention to the players as they began to chant, "Mel, Mel, Mel." The chanting increased as he worked his way through the book. As he shredded the last few pages the players broke into cheers. "It's the one thing I can do to get them psyched up," Mel explained.

Game day wasn't going well for LaVell Edwards. He had slept peacefully but after breakfast had developed a nagging headache. It wasn't a migraine, but a dull, steady pain in the back of his head—a daily temporary annoyance for him. But on this day he didn't want to be bothered by it.

The morning was filled with translucent sunlight, the skies turning overcast at times. A breeze swept across Mission Bay and at the rear of the plush hotel joggers silently plodded through their ritual on the green paths, the familiar screech of sea-gulls urging them on.

Edwards moved to the conference room for the last meeting. It was a boring, redundant exercise in habit, mostly a reminder of assignments they could follow in their sleep. They were advised of the times for team meal and bus departure and told to stay off their feet.

Not everybody complied.

Dan Plater, a pre-med student, was not disposed to sitting around staring blindly at soaps. Instead he spent part of the day with team doctor Brent Pratley, later sneaking away with friends from San Diego to go to the zoo. He lingered as long as he could, watching the bears. It was all so comfortable and he wondered aloud to a friend if he really wanted to play football that night.

Clay Brown looked at the clock beside the bed of the hotel room, then at his wife, Ria. Time to board the team bus. He eased his way out of his chair, kissing her and sauntering to the doorway with a wave.

A thought kept coming back to him. He remembered a dream Ria had the night before the 1979 Holiday Bowl against Indiana. She had dreamed he made the winning catch on the last play of the game.

He swung open the door, pausing at the threshold, one foot outside, and poked his head back in.

"Ria, remember the dream you had last year?"

She nodded.

"Maybe this time," he said.

Edwards had taken a nap in the afternoon to shake the headache, but he was wondering if it was going to return as the game started. Though Scott Phillips ran the first play of the game up the middle for an eight-yard BYU gain, two incomplete passes and a delay of game penalty forced a punt.

Then things got ugly.

SMU quarterback Lance McIlhenny ran for 12 yards and Craig James for gains of three and 22 yards, barreling over the arthritic-looking Cougars. Eric Dickerson went 15 yards for a touchdown and the game was 7-0 with barely two minutes gone. Most aggravating to the Cougars was the way SMU started: fanfare and muscle. The Mustangs didn't finesse their way across the goal line. There's no such thing as finesse in Texas. They went over the top.

McMahon threw a pair of incompletions, forcing a punt. On third down SMU's James faked a punt and ran 45 yards for a touchdown. Three minutes later a bad punt snap gave SMU a safety and a 16-0 lead halfway through the first quarter. Kicker Eddie Garcia, who already had two conversion kicks behind him, toed a 42-yard field goal for a 19-0 lead.

By then the largely pro-BYU crowd had begun to moan, as did some of the players, kicking the turf in frustration. Bill Davis stared angrily from the sidelines at his last college game. He caught sight of a Cougar cheerleader he had dated during the first semester and planned to see after the holidays.

"Danny," he said to Plater.

"Yeah?"

"I don't even want to show my face back at school."

In just over 10 minutes the Cougars had erased the pleasant memory of an 11-1 season, a national ranking and a win over the Big 10. They were in the tank.

Boos began to sift down from the upper tiers of the stadium as 50,214 people, most of them wearing blue, showed what they thought of losing another bowl game. Brown's mother, Betty McGinnis, left the stadium and began the drive home, saying she couldn't bear to see her son's face after another bowl loss.

BYU finally got on the scoreboard when Brown, sprinting down the sidelines, reached back and remarkably one-handed a catch by scooping it in near his hip for a 64-yard touchdown, closing the score to 19-7. Still, the Cougars blundered along. McMahon threw an interception and SMU worked its way to the BYU 3, aided by two Cougar penalties. James took a pass that made it 26-7 and Garcia kicked a 44-yard field goal for a 29-7 lead.

The Cougars stayed within striking distance due to freshman Via Sikahema's 83-yard punt return in the second period but even that was dampened when the conversion failed. The snap was off and, instead of kicking on the play, BYU's Bill Schoepflin fell short with a two-point conversion pass. BYU left the field at halftime trailing 29-13.

In the locker room Edwards calmly reminded his players how they had reached the Holiday Bowl, admonishing them not to embarrass themselves now. Though they were headed in that direction—two touchdowns and two field goals away from the lead —30 minutes remained in the game and Mustang all-America cornerback John Simmons was out after a first-half injury. A less experienced player would now take over a position crucial to stopping the BYU passing attack.

But the halftime hopes were no good. SMU's relentless running game was better in the second half than the first. Dickerson and James continued alternating at tailback, coming in fresh and punishing the tiring Cougar defense. James for 10, Dickerson for 28, James for 10. Then it was Dickerson for a yard up the middle and a 35-13 lead.

The crowd began to dwindle, many embittered at the prospect of another loss. While some players on the sidelines stood sullen and quiet, others joked about making the score respectable. Even after McMahon found Brown for a 13-yard touchdown with 6:40 left in the third quarter, the trickle of departing fans turned to a flood. The Cougars' curse all night, poor execution, stayed with them as they missed a second two-point conversion, freezing the score at 35-19. When Garcia kicked a 42-yard field goal, upping SMU's lead to 19 points, and McMahon was sacked to end the third quarter in despair, the crowd resorted to outright abandonment, emptying large sections of seats.

A quarter of the crowd was gone when the final period began, many moving off into the night in total disgust. Cougars were taunted by the SMU players who snarled, "Welcome to the Southwest Conference." In the lower stadium one Mustang backer wearing a cowboy hat and smoking a cigar bellowed, "BYU, what's that? What's the WAC? Maybe you ought to stick to playing Colorado State."

SMU punted early in the fourth period, turning the ball over to BYU on the Cougar 10. McMahon began clicking steadily on his passes, completing five straight before missing Braga on a third down play. It was fourth down, BYU trailing by 19 points and under eight minutes left.

Edwards called for the punting team. "I knew then it was over," Plater would say later. "It was obvious they had given up."

As the punting unit began moving onto the field, it happened. The offensive squad came off—all but McMahon. He stood, glaring at Edwards; Edwards shouted at him to get off the field. McMahon stormed closer to the sidelines, jaws working and face flushed, screaming: "What's the matter? Are you giving up now?"

McMahon wouldn't leave the field, forcing Edwards to call time out to avoid a delay-of-game penalty.

So there it stood. The Cougars humiliated, a quarterback in mutiny and, as Edwards reasoned, not much left to lose.

The offense went back in.

McMahon threw to Brown for a first down on a down-and-out pattern. The rhythm stayed with him, and he connected on five of his next six passes, including another fourth-down toss for a first down. Phillips sprinted around the left end for a touchdown that closed SMU's lead to 38-25, though again the two-point try failed.

Just over four minutes remained. Still only a wish.

The Mustangs struck with a thunderbolt that killed BYU's revived hopes on the next play from scrimmage. James, an imposingly strong and fast back, cut left after starting right and sprinted 42 yards for a touchdown and a 45-25 lead with 3:57 left to play.

Edwards grimaced, turning to assistant Dick Felt. "There goes any hope we had of winning," he sighed.

Instead, what followed was a comeback that has rarely been seen; a finish that moved some to call it the greatest bowl game ever; a comeback played before a half-empty stadium and an SMU band drifting onto the sidelines wearing silly red-and-white nightshirts, blaring horns and taunting the Cougar bench.

Even television announcer Ray Scott had pronounced the eulogy on the Cougars. "SMU has 45 points . . . and for BYU it turns out to be its third fruitless trip to the Holiday Bowl," he said.

McMahon moved the Cougars to SMU's 15 as the seconds ticked steadily away, firing a touchdown pass in the left corner to Matt Braga. To this day no photograph or film shows with certainty whether the ball skidded along the ground or not before reaching Braga. It was a catch McMahon would later term the greatest he had ever seen. The official waited several seconds on the play, appearing in need of someone to tell him if the pass was complete. Braga did just that.

With a low, outstretched dive, he plucked the ball away from a plunging SMU defensive back, coming up with the ball — not to mention an Academy Award performance — above his head in triumph. It was ruled a touchdown.

A missed two-point pass to Phillips again reminded the Cougars of their missed opportunities — the fourth failed conversion try of the night. The score stood 45-31.

Braga plopped down on the bench and Davis trotted over beside him, leaning to whisper in Braga's ear.

"Matt, you catch that ball?"

Braga gave him a "yeah, sure" grin.

"How many bounces?"

"I think only one. Two at the most."

Braga, apparently deciding too much talk could get him in hot water, told postgame interviewers he wasn't sure about the ball bouncing, but he thought he made the catch before it hit the turf.

The Cougars were rolling now, and they knew it.

Scovil walked near Edwards, saying, "We aren't going to win this but we'll make it close."

Under three minutes remained. Todd Shell recovered an onside kick and the crowd began to awaken, jolted out of its droning lethargy. The nearly audible sound of television sets clicking off in Utah had subsided as the Cougars suddenly mounted a bonafide comeback.

McMahon caught Davis between two defenders on a stunning 40-yard pass that ended at the SMU 1-foot line. Phillips swept around the right side untouched and caught a pass for the two-point conversion, making the score 45-39.

The brilliant comeback, even then, seemed futile. SMU's Dick Blaylock recovered BYU's desperate onside kick: all SMU had to do was eat up the last 1:57, an easy task for a running team like the Mustangs. But the BYU defense, grossly battered about much of the night, stopped Dickerson for a loss on the first play. McIlhenny went right for three. The Cougars used their last timeout with 1:06 left.

Dickerson came back to gain two. And slowly, maddeningly, the Mustangs got up, eating away the time as they walked back to the huddle. The seconds continued to tick away . . . 35 . . . 30 . . . 24 . . . 18 . . . A delay-of-game call moved the ball back.

Eric Kaifes dropped back for a punt he hoped would jam the Cougars deep in their own territory with no timeouts and too much ground to cover. Taking the snap, he stepped forward, swinging back for the kick and . . . blocked! Cornerback Bill Schoepflin had stormed in from the left side to smother the punt, turning it over to BYU.

McMahon missed Lloyd Jones in the end zone and on the next play purposely threw short to Brown, who was open in the middle of the field, knowing the clock would have run out had Brown caught the pass.

Then all there was left was a quarterback, a play that hadn't been used in any game in BYU history, and three seconds.

Tony Roberts strained to be heard over the sounds of the crowd as he called the game to a radio audience that stretched to the armed forces around the world. "And now it's third down and 10 from the 41 . . . This is it . . . Back to throw . . . last down (sic) . . . no time on the clock. It is . . . it is . . . what?"

Eric Lane ignored the orders to block from his running back position alongside McMahon, instead racing downfield to help with the catch. Scott Phillips stayed inside and, ironically, had to stop a blitzing linebacker who got past the line. Phillips brushed him aside just as McMahon brought back his arm.

Brown never veered, heading straight for the goalposts. The pass came in a high arching loft, drifting through the darkness as the noise closed in. Three players converged on Brown as he turned. Three other SMU defenders rushed toward him.

"CAUGHT!" shouted Roberts. "He caught it. Touchdown on the last play. Brigham Young has won it. A miracle catch. Everybody went up in the air for the football. I don't believe it . . . I don't believe it and yet I saw it!"

Indeed it was a miraculous catch: not that the play was difficult — Brown's one-handed stab in the first half was much tougher to execute — but that the ball found its way to Brown through all the arms. Moving into the end zone he saw the ball

*The end of the most storied play in BYU football history: Clay
Brown, surrounded by SMU opponents, leaps for the ball (top
left) and finds himself far from in control of it (top right). But
as jubilant teammates signal (above), Brown has wrestled it
away from four defenders before hitting the ground.*

Kurt Gunther (2) drills the winning PAT through the goalposts.

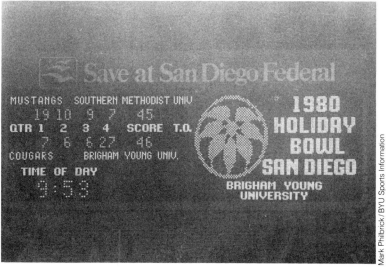

The scoreboard tells the improbable story of the "Miracle Bowl."

It all came down to McMahon's (9) arm and Brown's hands.

dropping from above, turned, facing the field, and leaped. His momentum carried him backward as Blaylock and Dwayne Anderson tracked the flight of the ball. Wes Hopkin went high over Brown's shoulder from behind, somehow falling short as Brown raised his hands above his head. Then he clutched the ball, pulling it frantically to his midsection, Hopkins's hands still on it as they fell in a jumbled heap.

Pandemonium. Edwards was staring upfield where McMahon had been, as if he hadn't seen the play. Actually, he had seen every dramatic second and was looking to make sure no penalty flags had been thrown. Through the commotion he turned to assistant Dick Felt and exclaimed dryly, "Well, at least we won't lose this one."

They lined up for the extra point kick, the score tied 45-45. Kurt Gunther carefully watched the snap to holder Bill Schoepflin, who bobbled it just as Gunther began his carefully timed stride. But Schoepflin recovered and spotted the ball, Gunther adjusting perfectly and arching his foot upward.

It was all over.

The Texan with the big hat turned to a row of people behind him, the cigar fallen from his lips and a stricken look on his face. "Here I am," he bellowed, holding his arms out in supplication. "Baptize me."

Edwards grabbed his head in disbelief as the game ended, laboring through the confusion to midfield where he shook hands with SMU Coach Ron Meyer. Mel, the manager, reached Edwards first, leaping on his shoulders. Plater was the first player to Edwards, throwing his arms around the coach's neck. A TV newsman stopped Edwards, pushing a microphone towards him. "I uh . . . I don't know, I just . . . shows . . . one of the most unbelievable things I . . . it's just . . . I don't know . . . it's like . . . I don't know, it's hard to say . . . I don't know. Thing is we made so many mistakes. I don't know," stammered the normally unflappable Edwards. He raised his hands in exasperation, shaking his head. "We killed ourselves all night long. We never gave up was the key."

Meanwhile McMahon, deluged by reporters and well-wishers, tried explaining the game's final pass. "Just a prayer," he said. "A Hail Mary pass."

The press elevator is one of the slowest things ever invented by man. A throng of journalists waited impatiently by the door, watching the interminable light over the doors go down, then rise a floor or two, then sink again.

Outside the open-air pressbox the jubilation had not yet died. This one had quickened even the pulses of a corps of sportswriters and sportscasters who had covered hundreds of football games. As Brown made his catch most stared in disbelief, straining to replay in their minds the exact sequence of the final play. Others laughed or shook their heads.

The elevator finally arrived on the ground floor underneath the concrete stadium, as echoes from above swept through the bleak corridors. The field lights were still on, players mingling in fragmented groups, many with tear-stained faces, trying to convince themselves it had really happened. McMahon's father bear-hugged him, shouting, "I'm proud of you son, I'm proud of you." Finally they cleared the field, moving up the tunnel at the north end of the stadium, crowding through the crush of reporters to the dressing-room door.

Inside, the door bolted, the team continued to celebrate, spraying soda around and screaming at anyone who cared to listen. Outside the media waited, fretting over deadlines.

The coaches tried to shout down the noise, pushing a deadline of their own to make the flight back to Salt Lake City before San Diego's curfew took effect. As the locker-room din subsided, shouts of jubilation still drifted softly down.

BYU President Jeffrey B. Holland stepped through the players to an open area of the room. "I've had some great heroes in my life," said Holland, explaining his admiration for some of the great figures of history. "Well," he continued, "I've just added another name to my list of heroes: The 1980 BYU football team."

The cheering ceased as Edwards moved to the center of the locker room. He stood, the room quiet, the players still sweating, each savoring the memory so that no detail would be lost in the years to come. For some there would be other games and other teams. For others it was the last game. Each knew it was a few seconds in a lifetime that they would always remember.

Still overwhelmed, Edwards looked around the room with a smile he may not have had since he was too young to remember. He shrugged his shoulders. "Well," he said, "what can you say about a win like that?"

A pause. Then came Davis's voice from one corner of the room.

"Hallelujah!"

2

Ainge's Dash

Wednesday afternoon's practice at the Providence Civic Center had quieted down as the players stood on the gleaming court watching BYU basketball coach Frank Arnold walk through a play. Danny Ainge stooped to pick up a basketball when it hit him: a sharp, paralyzing pain in his lower back.

He tried to straighten up but couldn't. Arnold continued his instructions without noticing Ainge, who had crouched, then gone slowly to the sidelines and gingerly sat down.

Arnold stopped talking and walked over with assistant Roger Reid to the hunched Ainge who sat with a puzzled look. "Hey, Danny, let's get up and get going," chided Arnold.

"Coach, my back hurts," was all Ainge said.

At first it looked like a joke. Though Ainge appeared aloof and distant to strangers, he was popular with teammates and was often joking. This, thought Reid for an instant, was another Ainge prank.

"I'm serious," said Ainge, reading the look in their faces. "It's really hurting."

And at that moment, so were the BYU Cougars.

The mood turned more serious. "Can't you finish it up?" said Arnold. Ainge shook his head. He tried to get up to shoot but couldn't straighten his back. Arnold told Ainge to go see the team trainer, Ollie Julkunen, in the training room, then moved back onto the court as the players gathered for the final moments of instruction. They were looking sideways at one another. Onlookers in the stands, who had come to get a glimpse of the Cougars in practice, craned their necks in curiosity as Ainge, crimped at the waist, cautiously worked his way under the stands.

Ten minutes later Arnold went to the training room and found Ollie, flanked by a trainer from Providence College, the host school of the 1981 NCAA East sub-regionals, shaking his head from side to side. "Coach, this is not good. Not good at all," said Julkunen in his thick Finnish accent.

Even then, there was no exceptional concern on the part of the coaches. Ainge had a history of little aches and pains but always, always he would come back in time to play the next game. But as Ainge's condition continued to worsen, so did their worries.

It was the eve of the first round of the NCAA playoffs in the Rhode Island city. BYU was to play Princeton the next night, the top team in the lightly regarded Ivy League. Though BYU had finished only third in the Western Athletic Conference that year, the Cougars had drastically improved at the season's end and beaten WAC co-champ Utah 95-76 in the final game of the year. Ainge had been outstanding, averaging over 24 points a game.

Providence was a long way from spring that

March 11. The Atlantic gales swept across brown lawns and through barren trees, dropping the wind-chill factor to near zero after dark. The Cougars were housed in a Holiday Inn, next to the Civic Center, so they could walk to practice. Down the street was a section of town dotted with Italian restaurants and neatly painted houses. Out their windows the players could see up the hill to the Rhode Island state Capitol and the buildings of Brown University.

BYU, Princeton, Georgetown, James Madison, Notre Dame and UCLA had been selected to play in Providence for the right to advance to the East Regional finals the next week in Atlanta. But all thoughts of Atlanta were shrouded in the gloomy expectation that Ainge, the soul of the team as well as its best player, would not play.

Ainge was never certain what caused his back spasms. He was laboring under the normal pressure that the playoffs bring, but pressure seemed to be made for a player like Ainge. He had played a frightening number of minutes that season, as Arnold could barely spare a play without Ainge there to run the team. He was the man with the ball most of the time, the top scorer and on BYU's successful 1-3-1 zone defense, the player in the most important position as he moved along the baseline picking off passes inside to start BYU's fast break. Some said it was fatigue, others tension and others that it was unrelated to basketball. The big concern wasn't what caused it, though, but how long it would last. "Danny was really scared," Reid would say later. "You could see it on his face."

Ainge returned to his room after the practice to lie on the bed, hoping the pain would ease, but the muscles continued to cramp. He skipped team dinner, having his meal brought up to the room.

Late into the night, long after roommate Steve Trumbo had gone to sleep, Ainge lay awake looking around the darkened room, his back throbbing.

As the night moved on, word of Ainge's injury spread. The news media caught wind quickly, as a number of reporters had been at the practice when Ainge left. And indeed it was significant news. With Ainge, Princeton was a poor match for the physical Cougars. Without him the teams were nearly even. And it was looking more and more like BYU would play without him.

The next morning phone calls began to flood in for Ainge and Arnold. Some were return calls from doctors and specialists Arnold and his staff had contacted. Others came in unsolicited, from chiropractors, psychiatrists, doctors, therapists and reporters. Word had also reached the bookies in Las Vegas, who were trying to get the straight story that might alter the betting line.

Calls came in from every imaginable point: Florida, California, Utah, Nevada, even New Zealand. Doctors and therapists talked to Ainge, suggesting various exercises, some of which he tried. None worked. He moved to a Providence hospital for treatment and a chiropractor later worked with him. No cure.

Early that morning, team physician Dr. Brent Pratley picked up the Los Angeles *Times* and read the news about Ainge. It was already nearing noon in Providence when Pratley phoned Arnold: "I'll be there at seven o'clock tonight," said Pratley.

"We're going across the street at seven-thirty to get ready for the game," Arnold replied.

The calls continued, but still there was no change. The team walked over at noon for a light shooting practice, conspicuously missing Ainge.

It was after six o'clock when Dr. Pratley knocked on Arnold's door at the Holiday Inn. Arnold spoke tersely with Pratley before they hurried down the hall. Stepping inside Ainge's room, they saw him lying flat on his back on the bed. Pratley examined him and then picked up the phone, calling a colleague in Los Angeles with the diagnosis. Arnold listened intently to the "one-way conversation" that lasted five minutes. Pratley hung up. "Go ahead and play him . . ." Pratley said cryptically, "if you want to destroy his career."

"That's an easy decision," Arnold replied, turning to Ainge. "Danny, you don't play. We can't risk your career."

Ainge blinked at the decision and then, as if to give it one more try, lifted his head, winced and slowly pushed himself off the bed. Bent over like a question mark he hobbled to the dresser and braced himself. He gave Arnold a pleading look but ·said nothing. He knew he couldn't play. It hurt too much.

At seven-fifteen Arnold told Ainge they were going to the arena in 15 minutes. "Do you want to come over and watch for awhile?" he asked.

"Yeah."

Ainge dressed slowly and sullenly before they stepped on the elevator, meeting the rest of the team in the lobby. They moved into the brisk night, walking around the side of the building towards the arena and across a wide expanse of sidewalk, their pace measured and deliberate not unlike a caravan of mourners, no one saying much as they trudged along. Reid leaned to Arnold. "No way. He's not going to play," he said quietly.

Even Ainge knew. There had been many aches, but they always disappeared once he got his adrenalin pumping. But this time it wasn't working. He had told his wife at the hotel that he wouldn't be able to play and was so certain of it that he didn't bother packing all his warmup things in his gym bag before leaving. "I kept waiting and waiting for him to say he'd play," said Reid. "But he never did."

The team sat in the stands watching the first game between Georgetown and James Madison while a chiropractor worked on Ainge's back, but he felt no better. Meanwhile Pratley had given Ainge pain killers and muscle relaxants.

Ainge went to the stands while his teammates filtered into the dressing room to get taped. Gradually, as he sat watching the early game, the pain in his back began to ease. Feeling slightly better, he went back to the locker room where the others were already dressing. "Coach, I feel kind of stupid sitting on the bench in my street clothes," said Ainge. "Do you mind if I put my warmups on and sit on the team bench?" Arnold just looked curious and nodded.

Ainge cautiously dressed, still not expecting to play. It was eight forty-five, 45 minutes before game time. The locker room was unusually quiet, the glum spell still over the team.

Arnold stepped to a chalkboard to begin his customary 15-minute meeting with the team. Ainge was paying no attention. His pain had decreased since Pratley had administered the medication, and he collared Ollie. He stretched out on the floor in front of Arnold, Ollie pulling and rubbing at his back. "There he is stretched out," remembers Arnold, "and the kids are watching, and I'm trying to draw Xs and Os, and I was kind of annoyed because Ollie and Danny are going through this darn thing and we're playing a pretty good ball club."

It went on for 15 minutes, Arnold talking but nobody listening, everyone watching Ollie's patient work. Then Arnold sent the team out to warm up, remaining behind, as was his custom, to think alone. Ainge got up and walked around a moment. "Coach, I'm feeling kind of limber. Would you mind if I went out and just shot some layups with them?"

Typical Danny, he thought.

"O.K., but don't do anything foolish."

"I won't, but I think I can do some easy layups."

Arnold remained in the quiet room for a few minutes. When he went out to the floor, there was Ainge, shooting layups and looking better than he had in 24 hours.

It was now 12 minutes before tipoff as Arnold stood on the edge of the court watching Ainge. In another two minutes they would go back into the dressing room for a few final words. Arnold had set his mind he wasn't going to play Ainge and he walked out on the court, taking Ainge by the arm.

"Danny —"

"Just let me try it!" Ainge interrupted.

"What are you talking about?" Arnold scolded.

"Lemme try it."

"Danny, it's your career. I cannot let you do that," Arnold argued, trying not to look too conspicuous to the crowd.

But Ainge wouldn't give in. "Coach, I know how important this is. I wouldn't do anything if I thought there was any problem at all. Let me try it. I'm loose. I feel good. *Let me try it!*"

They returned to the locker room. Ainge was bouncing a ball between his legs, moving around and grinning. Arnold gave some final instructions and they trotted under the stands and into the brightness of the court. As the teams lined up for the opening jump, standing there at the edge of the circle was, naturally, Ainge.

That the Cougars had made the NCAA tournament and were favored over Princeton was no consolation. Prior to that game BYU was 4-12 in NCAA playoff competition; only Connecticut, Wyoming and Miami of Ohio had worse playoff records among teams that had been invited four or more times.

Princeton, though, wasn't a problem. The Tigers were a deliberate, methodical team that usually plodded along slowly enough to stay close until late in the game, then got the lead and sat on it. But with Ainge playing they were no match for BYU.

Ainge took two missed jump shots and nearly five minutes playing time before he made his first basket. He was still tight, but definitely healing as he moved about, loosening up as the game progressed. His first basket came on a wheeling drive into the lane for a 10-foot jumper that tied the score at 8-8. He connected on an 18-footer three minutes later, moving BYU's lead to 15-10.

Princeton played its customary zone defense and carefully awaited high percentage shots on offense. At half BYU led 32-28 and both teams had shot over 60 percent from the field, a figure that reflected the caution the teams took in their shot selection.

Both teams cooled, however, in the second half — but by then Ainge was approaching full speed. He scored 13 second-half points, including eight of nine BYU points in a flurry that boosted the lead from three to nine. BYU never trailed in the second half.

Though the muscles began to stiffen again in Ainge's back after the game, the storm had passed. He wasn't going to miss any games, particularly since the next playoff opponent was a young, quick and nationally ranked team; a team, in fact, with the proudest past in college basketball history: UCLA.

Saturday's game against the Bruins was on national television, but despite the capacity crowd at the Providence Civic Center, there was at first only passive interest in the two western teams — particularly BYU. They had heard, of course, of the venerable string of national championships the Bruins had put together in the '60s and '70s, but several key players were only beginning their collegiate careers and would not become nationally familiar for some time.

It was an hour before game time when Cougar junior Fred Roberts, who had scored 19 points against Princeton, went out in his warmups to shoot with a couple of teammates. Only a few hundred people were in the stands. Newsmen were plugging in their computers while television crewmen scurried along the floor, stringing electrical cords and positioning cameras.

Roberts could hear voices in the near-empty bleachers asking just where this BYU team was from and who they beat to get to the playoffs. He turned just as a cheer went up near the other end of the court. The Bruins emerged and an appreciative *Oooohhhh* arose as the crowd sighted the familiar UCLA uniforms. Several fans called out to UCLA's "Rocket" Rod Foster, a Connecticut star before moving west for college.

And so it went, all somewhat irritating to the Cougars, hungry to prove themselves on a national scale. Though BYU had a respectable 24-6 record entering the game and was ranked No.'s 16 and 17 in the two major wire service polls, the Bruins were 20-7 and rated No.'s 10 and 11.

As the Bruins warmed up they cast only an occasional, unconcerned glance toward the BYU end of the court. UCLA was supposed to win with its speed, which the big, ponderous, white BYU team would likely be unable to neutralize.

But UCLA's quickness never entered the picture. The only picture that afternoon was the one of Ainge beating up on the proud Bruins all by himself. Suddenly UCLA was just another college basketball team. Ainge scored 23 of BYU's 31 first-half points, hitting five free throws and nine of 11 field goals. The halftime stats: Danny Ainge 23, UCLA 22.

On one remarkable first-half shot Ainge drove toward the lane, taking the ball over his head and leaping between two defenders, then brought the ball down and spun it underhand off the glass as the crowd screamed with glee. Two points. The passivity of the crowd in the early moments of the game had long since evaporated into chants for Ainge to shoot each time he touched the ball and, finally, calls of "Ainge! Ainge!"

He was equally phenomenal in the second half as the Cougars continued running over the embarrassed Bruins. Ainge ended the game — one of the greatest of his career — with 37 points. The final score smugly told the story: BYU 78, UCLA 55.

The nationally televised rout of UCLA turned BYU into a curious phenomenon. The Cougars were now among the "Sweet Sixteen" teams left in the tourney, yet had finished only third in their conference. They were the only team in the tournament without a single black player, a fact that made even the Cougar players self-conscious. And there was, of course, the Ainge story: the brilliant college player some reporters went so far as to call the best in the country that year; the same great college player who had already announced that he would not be starring in the National Basketball Association the next year, but playing baseball for the Toronto Blue Jays after the tournament. Ainge had been playing in relative obscurity until the tournament, but he was now in the middle of a spectacular March that would eventually lead to a consensus all-America and the College Player of the Year by two organizations.

"Now I know what became of Frank Merriwell," wrote Atlanta columnist Furman Bisher during the playoffs. "He's alive and well and spends the winters in Provo, Utah, wearing No. 22 and the summers in Toronto, Ont., wearing No. 2."

In a few quick days the mood of the BYU contingent had shifted from despair to exhilaration. Ainge's sore back was only a hazy memory. So was UCLA. BYU was a hot team, with the hottest player in the country.

On Wednesday the Cougars jetted loose into Atlanta for the East Regional finals. They were practicing loose and thinking loose. Their opponent for Thursday was Notre Dame, rated No.'s 7 and 9 in the two polls, a team with four starters that would go on to play in the NBA. But BYU had realized in beating UCLA that a high ranking didn't mean you couldn't beat 'em. Ainge was well, Roberts was playing the best basketball of his career and they had already outdone any expectations.

Notre Dame was exceptionally talented with all-America Kelly Tripucka, stocky, with a fine shooting touch from the perimeter, at one forward and Orlando Woolridge, a 6-foot-9 honorable mention all-America at the other side. Though Woolridge had been nursing a chronic charley horse in his thigh for several games, he was going to play against BYU. At center was 6-10, 230-pound Tim Andree and the guards were Tracy Jackson and John Paxson. It was the first time in the playoffs the Cougars, who started

6-10 Fred Roberts, 6-8 Steve Trumbo and 6-11 Greg Kite on the front line, would face as big and strong a lineup. Still, BYU coach Frank Arnold downplayed his team's success. "All we've got is a bunch of heavy-legged guys who can't jump a lick," he said.

The crush of media requests increased as the national press stormed Atlanta, looking for more to write about Ainge, as well as the young giant Ralph Sampson, whose Virginia Cavaliers had made the final 16, too. Many of the questions posed to the BYU players were oriented more toward religion than basketball: Do players have to serve two-year missions? Does BYU actively recruit blacks? Is basketball a missionary effort at BYU?

Meanwhile Arnold, who had had his periods of disenchantment with press and officials in the WAC, charmed many eastern reporters with his straightforward sincerity. They called him "refreshingly candid," and, having never dealt with him before, found him surprisingly approachable. Some even sought Arnold out for information about religious doctrine.

The BYU-Notre Dame game was to be held on Thursday night, along with the Virginia-Tennessee game, in The Omni, a futuristic arena that had sold out all 15,461 seats. It was to be televised across most of the nation.

Although the Cougars had shown few signs of feeling the pressure of the playoffs during the week, they were tight when the game started. The Irish were a team used to dictating the pace but, unlike Princeton, had the talent to stay with virtually any opponent. While the Cougars were tentative, rarely moving into the successful fast-break offense, Notre Dame controlled the tempo. BYU was preoccupied with out-thinking the Irish.

Whatever Ainge had been the first two games, he wasn't against Notre Dame. The Irish had gone to a box-and-one defense, putting Paxson on Ainge with instructions to dog him even when he didn't have the ball. Part of the time there were two people on Ainge, rendering him unable to control the offense as he was accustomed to. In the first half Ainge only got off four shots, missing them all, and he had but two free throws to his credit by the end of the first half. What's more, nobody else was hitting and Notre Dame built a 28-18 halftime lead, the Irish having made half their shots while BYU could make only 32 percent of its field goal tries. Notre Dame had appropriated most of the breakaway abandon that had distinguished the Cougars earlier in the tournament.

Though BYU trailed by 10 at halftime and was shooting poorly, there was some optimism because the Irish had been unable to break the game open. Arnold chided his team for allowing Notre Dame to control the game's pace, a strategy that had accounted for BYU's success that year. "Just chuck everything!" Arnold scolded. "Just play street ball with them. All I want you to do is freelance and do things instinctively, just as if you were playing five-on-five in the middle of the summer."

It had been a strong defensive game, so much so that players were hesitant to shoot for fear of missing. And now, in midstream, they were being told to play an everybody-gun-it-up street game.

Still, there was no noticeable change as the second half began. Though BYU's shooting percentage improved, the Irish were slowly pulling away. Tripucka drove the baseline for a 30-18 lead to open the scoring and followed with an 11-foot jump shot for a 14-point lead, the biggest of the game. The crowd lapsed into a monotone as it began losing interest. Now all the Irish had to do was lie back and wait it out, an attitude that coach Digger Phelps would soon find cost his team not only its momentum, but the game.

So early in the second half Notre Dame began holding the ball, waiting for easy shots. The shots never came and BYU started creeping back. Roberts scored three straight baskets and Ainge hit a free throw, closing Notre Dame's lead to six points. When Woolridge was called for goal tending with 7:34 left in the game, the Irish called time out in hopes of slowing BYU's momentum. The lead had been cut to 44-40. But a flurry of Notre Dame fouls had put the Cougars in the bonus situation, forcing the Irish to play cautious defense. Greg Ballif drove for a layup, drew a foul and hit it, cutting Notre Dame's lead to 48-47. On the play Jackson had fallen to the ground and the 250-pound BYU center Greg Kite had accidentally stepped on his head. Jackson was helped off the court and replaced by Tom Sluby.

BYU's advantage gained by the loss of an Irish starter was negated with 1:43 to go when Roberts fouled out. Woolridge missed and with 1:01 left in the game BYU took its first lead of the game when Ballif sank an 18-foot, I-can't-believe-he-did-that shot for a 49-48 lead.

The crowd was standing and roaring as Notre Dame worked the ball across midcourt, calling time with 52 seconds left. Bringing the ball in bounds, they nervously passed it around the perimeter, calling time out again with 24 seconds to set up a final play.

In BYU's huddle there was some confusion over what to do. Assistant coaches Harry Anderson and

Roger Reid had suggested a zone defense to keep the Irish away from an inside shot, a change from the man-to-man they had been successfully using. Arnold said no, speculating that Notre Dame would go to Tripucka and he wanted somebody "tagging him all the time. I won't risk the zone," said Arnold.

Trumbo cut in saying he would dog Tripucka because at 6-foot-8 he would be able to shut him down, but Arnold nixed that saying to do so would leave the 6-foot-4 Ballif on 6-9 Woolridge and surely they would go inside for a mismatch. Arnold said they would put Ballif on the 6-6 Tripucka, man-to-man.

True to Arnold's hunch Notre Dame brought the ball in, passing it to Tripucka as the seconds ticked away, Ballif working on him. Tripucka dribbled to the right corner and put up what was supposed to be the shot of the tournament. The clincher. An 18-foot fall-away jumper with Ballif right in his face. The shot went down with eight seconds to go. BYU called time out, 94 feet from the basket and hoping there was time for one last shot.

Arnold looked up at the huddle of faces before him as he began setting up the final play. An instantaneous feeling of despair at Tripucka's basket showed in their eyes. But as they checked the clock while walking back to the bench for the timeout they began considering what could be done in eight seconds. Some of the players would say later they had a feeling all along they would pull off the win. Others weren't kidding themselves about their chances. "People aren't honest when they say, well, I know we're gonna win this thing," Ainge says, "You're thinking, well, it's not over, but if I were a betting man, I'd bet against it. On the other hand, I knew there was a chance to win."

And the chance rested — as everyone in the arena knew — on the shoulders of Daniel Ray Ainge.

If Notre Dame came out in a zone, hanging back to keep away the inside shot, Ainge was to drive as far as he could and take the jumper at the foul line or pass to an open man underneath if there was time. If they went man-to-man, which the Cougars didn't expect, Ainge was to take his man one-on-one and get the best shot he could. Neither Ainge nor the coaches expected anything better than a 15-foot jump shot and they doubted the Irish would risk containing Ainge by going man-to-man.

But when they broke their huddles, Notre Dame was showing a man-to-man.

Steve Trumbo had been enjoying the moment, looking up into the frantic crowd during the timeout and soaking in the drama, until the players spread onto the court for the inbounds play. Then it struck him.

"Danny, I wasn't listening," he said to Ainge with a half sheepish, half panic-stricken voice. "What am I supposed to do?"

"Don't worry about it," said Ainge. "Just get the ball to me."

The crowd was on its feet as the referee handed the ball to Timo Saarelainen under the Irish basket. Ainge looped from the foul line to near the baseline, taking Saarelainen's pass, Paxson pounding after him. Then Ainge turned up court along the sideline and began the drive that would be replayed a thousand times, a drive that would erase the memory of a poor day in which Ainge would only score 12 points. But the last two of those points would be the biggest of his career.

On a dead sprint Ainge moved beyond Paxson, but closing in on him at midcourt were Tripucka and Sluby to head him off. Ainge, without breaking stride, slipped between the two, taking the ball behind his back as he angled toward the free-throw line.

Two men and four seconds left.

Shifting the dribble from one hand to the other he faked right on Tim Andree, the big center, at the foul line.

And then all there was between Ainge and the hoop was Orlando Woolridge, guarding the basket with his life.

Ainge went straight at Woolridge, softly arching the ball with an underhand layup. Woolridge jumped at the same instant, his hand briefly catching the net as he went up, which slowed his acceleration

Danny Ainge gets past Tim Andree (left) and goes up . . .

the shot barely clearing the reach of Orlando Woolridge . . .

before a moment of waiting (left), and then the celebrating.

some—a factor that may have saved Ainge's basket. The ball drifted toward the hoop, clearing Woolridge's fingertips by not more than two inches and nestled in the basket as the buzzer went off.

The entire BYU bench, along with much of the crowd, flew off their seats, leaping and screaming at the last shot. The 10 players on the court had frozen for a heartbeat at the buzzer, looking for the referee's signal that the basket was good. Ainge sprinted out from the baseline, jumping and laughing, as the deafening sounds rained from the stands. Ainge made a circle on the floor, shaking his right fist triumphantly while teammates pounded his back and hugged each other, then charged down the corridor to the locker room.

The confusion continued to wash over the court in waves. Across from where Ainge had made his shot, Tripucka knelt on one knee, weeping, his tears splashing on the floor. He raised his head slowly, looked disbelievingly at the score—BYU 51, Notre Dame 50—and dropped it again in anguish. People were spilling onto the floor, moving respectfully around Tripucka as a television camera closed in on him.

"When he got by those two players at half court I knew it was in," Assistant Coach Reid was saying excitedly. "It was in all the way. I knew it. There was no doubt in my mind. It was over."

Inside the locker room BYU's team was shouting and piling on top of Ainge, who was already thinking ahead. "We've got to get ready for Virginia," he was yelling, but nobody paid attention.

When the press moved in the screaming subsided, but the euphoria remained. "He was coming down and then he dribbled the ball behind his back and I'm going, 'I can't believe it,' " said Trumbo, holding audience with a group of reporters. "And then we were all jumping up and down and celebrating."

Notre Dame Coach Digger Phelps spoke quietly of the last basket in a tone of resignation. "We tried to stop him," he said. "But he's just too good an athlete. He reads so well that he just went to the opposite direction, got the ball and took it down the floor, right through five people."

The Notre Dame locker room was still, only an occasional curse or the muffled sounds of a quiet interview breaking through. "I thought . . . Dang, it's over," explained Woolridge to newsmen. "Not just the game. My college career. It's strange to see it all snap—everything—in six seconds. At first I just wanted to run out of the place. But then I knew I had to keep my composure and congratulate the other team."

Two days later the dream ended at the feet of 7-foot-4 Ralph Sampson and the Virginia Cavaliers, who moved on to the Final Four. Ainge, on the merits of his television hard sell in the playoffs, was named College Player of the Year.

BYU had gone farther in NCAA play—to the final eight—than any Cougar team in history. Many would quickly forget the up-and-down conference season, the UCLA game and 39 minutes and 52 seconds of the Notre Dame game. But few who saw have forgotten Ainge's drive through five Irish players and into BYU sports history.

3

This Time the Bride

Richard Zokol waved his club over the ball like a divining rod probing for water. Not far away, some of his BYU golf teammates were quietly celebrating the victory that awaited only his rubber-stamp shot.

The Cougars' long-sought-for NCAA championship was in the bag. Zokol faced a demanding sand shot from an oak-shaded bunker aside Stanford Golf Course's 18th green. But he couldn't give away BYU's three-shot lead — could he?

Coach Karl Tucker's face wasn't saying. The weatherworn eyes under his floppy hat had seen plenty of sun, 20 BYU golf teams and a handful of near-misses at NCAA tournaments.

Right now, celebrating was for the young. The man whose memory of such moments spanned two decades knew something could still go wrong. Deep down inside he knew it wouldn't, but . . . Why, just today Utah State's Jay Don Blake seemed to be a shoo-in for the individual title, but saw a big five-stroke lead disappear in a hurry.

Such is golf, and Tucker knew it. Zokol couldn't protect BYU's lead by dribbling the ball in circles to run the clock out. Nor could he drop to one knee behind a huge, protective offensive line. He had to hit a small, dimpled ball with a curved metal blade toward a hole barely large enough to fit your hand into. The mechanics alone were frightening.

Zokol methodically planted his feet into the sand as if into cement. The sand wedge finally stopped waving, coming to rest just behind the ball. He looked up once more at the flag that marked his target, then back down at the missile he hoped would fly the proper direction and length.

Tucker continued his uninterrupted study of the young golfer who might put the capstone on the crowning achievement of his coaching career. Oh, if he could just use that intense gaze to will a good shot here . . .

Karl Tucker could appreciate Dick Zokol's systematic plotting of the sand shot. Such had been his own rise to this moment.

BYU wasn't expecting a national championship when it hired the Olympus Junior High School teacher/coach to take over its golf program in 1961. All it wanted was a competitive team to represent the school well, and thus help achieve the goal of a more well-rounded athletic program.

But Tucker had loftier plans. He wanted a team that could compete with, and beat, any other squad in the country. Oh, and yes, an NCAA title.

There were some rather formidable obstacles blocking Tucker's noble intentions. Golf was dominated by Sun Belt schools, and for good reason. While courses in Utah were covered by snow, courses in California and Texas were covered only by sunshine. More practice opportunities would surely mean better players. And wouldn't the top players naturally gravitate to schools where they could more constantly hone their skills?

Not that top golfers were all that easy to find, anyway. High school and junior golf programs in many parts of the country were still in the formative stages. Top-quality, collegiate-level golfers were probably tougher to find than good quarterbacks. (Good prep golfers who were also members of the LDS Church were particularly scarce.) Competition to get them was, naturally, fierce. Combine this paucity with BYU's demanding standards and snow-bound winters, and . . .

It was obvious Tucker needed two things before hitting the road in search of his goals. One was a liberal travel budget that would allow his team to compete yearly in the top golf tournaments, particularly in California, while winter weather buried Provo. This was granted him — in ever-increasing amounts.

Second, he needed to possess the skills of a top recruiter, to work long and hard to sell BYU's fledgling golf program. Until it started rolling, he'd also have to sell Karl Tucker.

The first major "buyer" was Buddy Allin. He was soon followed by a dashing, blond-haired kid from California by the name of Johnny Miller. The plan was beginning to take shape.

Tucker didn't get his first major tournament win until 1966 — the Western Athletic Conference championship. But even with a fine nucleus of Allin and Miller, the Cougars still weren't considered a top national team. More depth was needed and Tucker set out to get it.

It came, and so did the tournament victories, in bunches, culminated by a stunning third-place

finish at both the 1969 and 1970 NCAA championships.

BYU golf had arrived. After eight years, Tucker
presided over probably the top non-Sun Belt golf
program in the nation. But it wasn't *the* number
1 — yet.

Tucker's reputation as a top-notch golf coach
began preceding him as he would set out to recruit
good golfers for his program. And they came to BYU
in ever-increasing numbers. Rarely did a BYU team
of the '70s lack a genuine star *and* depth. The
school's quadrennial revolving door began turning
out professional golf tour-qualified players almost
every year. Mike Brannan, John Fought, Mike Reid,
Pat McGowan, Bobby Clampett, Jim Nelford and
Jimmy Blair, to name a few, wore Cougar colors
during this era.

And the results showed. Only once was BYU out
of the top 10 at the NCAAs during this decade, including a string of top five finishes in 1975-80.

If the Cougar golf program had "arrived" in
1970, it had long matured into a consistent, potent
NCAA force by 1980. And arguably, it was the BYU
sports team best able to consistently compete with
success against the nation's top teams.

High school coaches, junior golf officials and former players now shaped an informal, but intricate
national scouting network. They would often call the
BYU coach with hot prospects they wanted to see
play for him. Tucker now presided over a well-
organized, self-perpetuating program that was considered a model among his coaching peers. His ability
to produce top teams and professional golfers year-in
and year-out in Provo was seen as a feat akin to the
pioneers' making a Great Basin desert bloom into a
burgeoning metropolis.

But Tucker's success wasn't merely organizational. He was greatly admired by just about every person to play for him. Rare was the week when "Heber," as he was known to his students, didn't get at least a few calls from alumni to report on recent activities and successes or find the answer to a struggling golf game. An elegant gold watch was Johnny Miller's token of thanks to his coach. But virtually every other BYU golf professional, and several others as well, gave Tucker a regular gift. They sacrificed (and still do) a few days every other year to flock to Provo, at their own expense, to participate in Cougar Golf Day, a combination reunion, fund raiser and standing tribute to Tucker's relationship with his former students. Other golf coaches shook their heads in disbelief and amazement at the incredible success of these regular, family-like gatherings, and the devotion it demonstrated of the "boys" for their "Papa."

But as Karl Tucker entered his 20th year of coaching, there was just one thing this crack program and its fine players, including 11 first-team all-Americans, had yet to produce for him: that NCAA championship. A 20-year-long plan wouldn't be complete until he had one.

As Zokol heightened what little drama remained with his marathon pre-shot planning, Tucker could have almost taken the time to reflect on every one of the 20 teams in his coaching career. He might have chuckled to himself — the quintet before him was probably one of the least likely of his last dozen powerhouse squads to win a national championship.

Why, just the year before, 1980, his Bobby Clampett-led group had almost won the title. Clampett, one of the most honored college golfers of all time, had almost single-handedly taken his team out of the race with a horrible second-round 80 on Ohio State University's Scarlet Course. But two days later, he spearheaded a Cougar charge from four strokes back until BYU actually held the final-round lead after 12 holes. It was then that Oklahoma State played what Tucker still considers some of the most brilliant team golf down the stretch he's ever seen to wrest the title from BYU.

In 1979, at wind-swept Winston-Salem, North Carolina, Bobby Clampett and crew once more held a brief lead during the final round before fading to fourth place by the end of the tightly bunched tournament. Ohio State, like the weather most of the week, stormed from fifth place on the final day to win — or, more aptly, survive — the tournament.

Then there was the 1976 team, which another prominent college coach called "the best college golf team in history." (Mike Reid, Jim Nelford, Pat McGowan, Jimmy Blair, Mike Brannan and John Fought — all professional tour-qualified players.) BYU stood in second place, seemingly poised and ready to strike, after each of the first three rounds.

Then, early in the final round, they made their long-awaited charge. After eight holes the Cougars had pulled into a tie for the lead, with Oklahoma State once again, after having made up six shots from the round's start. But that momentum was quickly dashed on the par-5, 505-yard ninth hole at the University of New Mexico's South Course. BYU quickly fell back thereafter and finished seven shots in arrears of Oklahoma State (though still in second place). This time, OSU's championship was due more to BYU's poor play over the last nine holes (11 over par) than its own great shot-making.

Never, then, had a BYU team taken Tucker closer

to an NCAA championship than right now. And somehow it seemed fitting that this year's workman-like group, not the star-studded teams of the past, would be the one to do it.

As Zokol began to lift his club backwards in a steady, ascending arc, Tucker *knew* what the result would be. This team *was* different than the others, and destiny would finally marry it to an NCAA title.

Destiny—maybe that was it. Something extra must have lifted this team above the adversity it faced all year.

First was the matter of Bobby Clampett, or rather, the lack of him. He was to have returned for a much-anticipated senior season but chose to begin a professional career instead. Because of Clampett's individual brilliance and dominance, BYU was known as "Snow White and the Seven Dwarfs." Now that Snow White had met his "prince," the dwarfs were left to emerge from his shadow and tarry on alone.

One of those "dwarfs," promising sophomore John Bodenhamer, contracted potentially fatal Hodgkin's disease and had to be sent home to Washington for treatment early in the season. Then, in October 1980, former player Jack Chapman died of lymphatic cancer at the age of 31. It was a shock to a golf community that perceived itself as a family.

Several other 1980-81 team members endured worrisome maladies during the season. It was thought for a while that freshman Robert Meyer had diabetes. Senior Barry Willardson was hospitalized late in the season with an unrelenting staph infection. Junior Keith Clearwater had an abscess on his arm that required surgical removal.

But one trial seemed to have an overpowering impact on these young golfers. Tucker's wife (and, thus, the mother of this golfing "family"), Joanne, suffered kidney failure during the winter and had to have a replacement organ implanted in February. For several weeks team members were forced to fly on "automatic pilot" while their coach cared for his ailing wife.

What was already an unusually close-knit team, drawn together by a need to compensate for Clampett's absence, jelled and matured into an even more cohesive unit. "Honestly, we didn't have the talent of some other BYU teams of the past," concedes Dave DeSantis, one of two seniors on the NCAA tournament team. "But for some reason we meshed. There was a lot of friendship among us. We didn't quarrel, and that's a bit unusual for a golf team. We were all like brothers."

Zokol, the team's other senior, agrees. "I've talked to [fellow Canadian and ex-BYU golfer] Jim Nelford about it, and I'm convinced several other BYU teams had better individual talent than this one did. But we developed a bond my senior year. With Bobby Clampett leaving and John Bodenhamer's illness, our team meetings became very emotional. This closeness—I'd never experienced anything like it before. I think it was a driving factor in our success. There was something extra there."

It was unusual chemistry, then, that formed this team: the loss of a team leader, a natural camaraderie, illness, even death in the "family," and a knowledge that no one individual on this team would be able to carry the others.

All of these factors probably contributed to the group's rebound from an inconsistent fall season at generally less demanding tournaments to a fabulous spring campaign against top-notch competition. But surely, and demonstrably, they molded these practitioners of a highly individual sport, who were nicknamed "dwarfs" by a national golf magazine, into a first-rate team.

Make that *Team,* with a capital T. Because for the first time Tucker could remember, this group of Cougars, now on the verge of an NCAA title, didn't produce a single individual champion in the 13 tournaments they competed in. The Team, yes—it reaped six first places going into the NCAAs, including four at some of the nation's tougher spring tournaments. The Team was on a roll and rated No. 1 going into the national meet, but nary a coach queried before the tournament rated BYU a top favorite. The Cougars were usually mentioned among a second wave of teams that could possibly sneak in and win the title. And the unglamorous adjectives "solid," "consistent," "steady" and "well-coached" usually accompanied the word "BYU." From such assessments, it was hard to believe these same coaches had rated the Cougars No. 1 in their final poll.

Tucker seemed to recognize this reality when he said the week before the tourney: "It's a nice compliment to be ranked number one in the nation, but we're far from being an overwhelming favorite."

Who doesn't naturally overlook a basketball team whose starters all average between 10 and 12 points a game? But that's the kind of team BYU was. The top *seven* (of which only five were able to compete in the NCAAs) golfers had seasonal averages differing less than two strokes.

So while BYU proudly carried its No. 1 ranking and this incredible balance to the NCAA meet, it was hardly the talk of the tournament.

Just who were these unheralded golfers?

Barry Willardson, a junior from Houston. Willardson, a returned missionary (San Diego Mission), was the team's third-best golfer going into the NCAAs, but was fresh from a second-place tie at the WAC Championships. He was a quiet, consistent long-hitter.

Dick Zokol, a senior from Vancouver, British Columbia. Zokol drove all night from his Canadian home for a tryout with the BYU team after he had been recommended to Tucker by former Cougar golfer Jim Nelford. Zokol was a light-hearted practical jokester who didn't much care for schoolwork. He was also coming off a mediocre season made much more palatable by his tie with Willardson for second at the WAC meet. He was the Cougar most prone to streak shooting.

Dave DeSantis, a senior from Tucson, Arizona. DeSantis was a late addition to the NCAA squad after it appeared freshman Robert Meyer had earned the spot because of fine late-season play. DeSantis had had a somewhat disappointing senior season, but the team felt his experience and maturity would be an asset at the big meet. The even-keeled, quiet golfer had shown an ability to play well at big tournaments (witness his third-place finish against mostly professionals at the previous year's Utah Open).

Keith Clearwater, a junior from Rancho Murieta, California. If the Cougars had a leader on the course, he was it. Through steady play that included three second-place finishes during the regular season, Clearwater was named the Western Athletic Conference's Player of the Year. The LDS Church convert had transferred to BYU from St. Mary's in California at the urging of old buddy and junior golf teammate Bobby Clampett.

Richard Fehr, a freshman from Seattle, Washington. Fehr was most successful in his first year at

Mark Philbrick/BYU Sports Information

Dick Zokol, whose second-day birdie binge led the Cougar charge.

Rick Fehr was BYU's "awe-struck younger brother," but also a key team member.

Mark Philbrick/BYU Sports Information

Coach Karl Tucker waited 20 years for his first NCAA title.

Mark Philbrick / BYU Sports Information

BYU's Western Athletic Conference-winning team (from left):
Coach Karl Tucker, Rick Fehr, Keith Clearwater, Dick Zokol,
Dave DeSantis, Kent Kluba, and Robert Meyer. Kluba and
Meyer did not play with the team at the NCAA tournament, but
still contributed to the Cougars' amazing balance all season.

BYU, compiling the team's second-best seasonal
stroke average. He was also BYU's most consistent
golfer, finishing out of the top 10 in only one of his
14 tournaments. Through all this, Fehr quietly
stayed in the background, playing an "awestruck
younger brother role," says Tucker.

Not a big star in the bunch. Only one (Zokol) has
gone on to the professional tour so far. But there was
a formula working—and working much better than
anyone anticipated.

Barry Willardson sat in front of a microphone
with ESPN television commentators as Zokol began

his backswing from the sand trap. He was trying to make sense while emotions ran rampant through him. He thought he heard himself telling viewers that Zokol was pretty sure coming out of traps, and that a bogey would be okay here since the Cougars led by three strokes.

Then Zokol's club struck the ball and Willardson suddenly found himself talking to the little white object emerging from the spray of sand and flying toward the flag.

"Bite!" Willardson exclaimed to the ball, and the nation.

The BYU team almost did bite — the dust — during the first round. As expected, the Cougars demonstrated their extraordinary depth and consistency, but, unfortunately, it was the wrong kind. The five shot a "straight": 72 (Fehr), 73 (Clearwater), 74 (DeSantis), 75 (Willardson) and 76 (Zokol), none good enough to match or beat the Stanford Golf Course's par of 71.

And since only the top four scores are counted in the NCAA team tally, Zokol's 76 was tossed out and BYU was left with a 294, 10 over par. But the most discouraging thing the BYU team saw as it left the stately Stanford course after its mediocre round was how far down in the pack it was — and how far behind the leader.

Oral Roberts, which did have a "star" in Joe Rassett, rode that senior's sizzling 66 to a team score of 286, eight strokes in front of the Cougars.

But also ahead of or tied with BYU was fellow WAC member New Mexico, perennial powerhouse Houston, pre-tournament favorite Arizona State, Texas A&M, Texas and Georgia.

Let's make one thing clear, though. This was no county putt-putt that had taken the measure of BYU this day, or would extract its pound of flesh from every other team before the tourney was over.

This was *The* Golf Course at *The* Leland Stanford Junior University. It was designed and built in 1928-29 for $244,409 (a tidy sum at that time) by Billy Bell, who also put his touch on the breathtaking Pebble Beach layout. For years it had been rated among *Golf Digest*'s Top 100 U.S. courses. Then money-saving maintenance shortcuts began to take their toll and the course became easier to play and less respected.

But tradition is tradition, and the 18 holes that waited to devour 186 NCAA golfers in 1981 had been restored to much the same condition as those that gave college competitors fits in two prior generations (1966 and 1948). Five new bunkers had been added, more trees had been planted, large mounds suddenly appeared, fairways were once again narrow, and rough surrounding them forbidding. Even the old "constants" that had watched these changes over the years—300 large oak trees—seemed more intimidating.

Intimidation. If the Stanford name didn't do it, surely its golf course would. A San Francisco *Examiner* columnist said it seemed appropriate that the golfer teed off from the first hole and went downhill from there. At 6,776 yards it wasn't overwhelmingly long. But if you couldn't hit a tee shot straight or play from the fairway to generally small greens with a high degree of accuracy, a bogey (at least) could be your fate on almost every hole.

It humbled the golfer at every turn. While the breathtaking view from the 11th and 18th tees made golfers feel they could drive the ball all the way to San Francisco (which loomed in the distance), reality quickly set in when an exacting second shot had to be converted to have even a hint of a chance at a birdie.

So while the Cougars' situation looked gloomy — eight strokes back, well-buried in the pack and on an unforgiving course — Karl Tucker remained ever the optimist.

And as he sat down with his team for a special meeting that Wednesday night, he knew he had the solution that would turn it all around the following day. Tucker had taken notes on the course and wasn't happy with the way his players had approached four or five holes.

"I wasn't very gentle with them," he says. "I pretty much told them, 'Look guys, here's how you're going to do it tomorrow.'"

The problem holes were the fourth, where San Francisquito Creek had cost BYU several penalty strokes the first round, and the 11th, where Cougar golfers, thinking they could drive it long, frequently found the sand traps guarding both sides of the fairway.

Tucker convinced his golfers that they were playing well and that just a few changes in their *approach* to the course would mean much better scores on Thursday.

But even Tucker may not have been prepared for what was about to happen. BYU, cursed with a late tee time, faced harder, drier greens than the teams starting early. But the team still went out and shot a sparkling 4-under-par 280, a 14-stroke improvement on the first day's total. It would be the only sub-par round *any* team would manage during the entire tournament.

Better yet, it vaulted the Cougars into a five-stroke lead over Texas A&M and six over Oral Roberts and Houston, the two teams they knew they'd eventually have to outshoot for the title. About half of that 14-stroke difference came on the two holes Tucker had mapped out in detail for his players the night before.

Leading the way, and rebounding from his first-round, non-counting 76, was Zokol. His 5-under 66 included an incredible string of five straight birdies through the middle of the tough back nine.

It all started on No. 12 (he began his round on the back nine) after he'd made two ordinary pars, giving no hint of the impending explosion. The 5-foot putt for birdie there was followed with a 12-footer on No. 13, an extremely tough, breaking 25-footer at No. 14, a 20-footer on No. 15, and an inches-long tap-in after a great sand shot on No. 16. An 18-foot putt on the 18th hole that would have given him an astounding 29 after nine holes just skimmed the edge of the cup.

Zokol says it's still the most exciting stretch of golf he's ever played. "I wanted to ride it as far as it would go. It was one of those ultimate highs in golf when you know you are in absolute control. It doesn't happen very often."

Zokol lost his chance for an immortal round by playing even-par golf the rest of the way (one birdie, one bogey). His 66 would be recognized as merely great, and, along with Oral Roberts' Joe Rassett's first-round 66, the best individual effort of the tournament.

The senior didn't lead BYU to first place by himself. Fehr shot a 2-under 69, a round that was the epitome of steadiness (two birdies, 16 pars). And Clearwater matched par at 71, a score that looked better and better to players as the week progressed. Only DeSantis, who matched his first-round 74, and Willardson, at 78, escaped the scoring epidemic invading the BYU team.

Thursday's team gathering was a lot happier, and Tucker, as anxious to prevent breeding overconfidence in his players as keeping them believing in themselves after the first round, allowed himself a "nice round, guys."

BYU was again assigned a late tee time on Friday, but after Thursday's round, that didn't carry its usual stigma. Besides, the Cougars had a hidden emotional weapon that would help them bury the rest of the field. There, in the flesh and rooting the Cougars on, was Johnny Miller.

Miller had flown in from Washington, D.C., after an injury had forced him to withdraw from the Kemper Open. Sure, other former Cougar players— Tom Costello, Jamie Edman and Jimmy Blair—had been there offering moral support. But this was an unexpected boost from a man who had won nearly $2 million golfing and was one of the sport's most charismatic personalities. He had come hoping to see something he could never be a part of—an NCAA championship.

Unfortunately, it was the Cougars, not their opponents, who were spooked by the prestigious booster. At the round's halfway mark, BYU had not only frittered away its lead, but stood one stroke in back of Oral Roberts and four behind Houston. Once again, the wrong kind of consistency had been found —the entire team was shooting 10 over par poorly over the front nine.

But rather than sliding further, the team inexplicably began shooting better. That would be some feat if everyone were playing together. But in college golf, teammates are strung along consecutive holes and have little or no contact with their colleagues during the round.

The turnabout was almost magical. By the time the Cougars' final golfer had finished the 11th hole, they had their lead back, and would hold it — albeit slimly — for the rest of the afternoon.

BYU didn't play spectacularly on the back nine (2-over-par), but was just good enough to stay in front on a day when mediocrity afflicted the entire field. Only Utah State broke 290 as a team, and it was still 15 shots back and out of the title race. Zokol again led the team, this time with a 72. Willardson's 74, and 75s by DeSantis and Clearwater, were the other counting scores.

Though the Cougars shot their worst round of the four-day tournament — 12-over-par 296 — only Oral Roberts and Houston were able to gain ground among the frontrunners. ORU now stood only one stroke off the pace and Houston was four shots back.

The other Cougars (from Houston) would also have been just one shot away from BYU had not one of their golfers made a costly mistake. That error, and its outcome, engulfed otherwise placid Stanford Golf Course in a swirl of controversy that sucked in both the front-running Cougar teams.

Houston golfer Ray Barr was about to shoot from the rough surrounding the 14th green when he accidentally dropped his putter on the ball. The ball hopped about four feet closer to the green. That's a one-shot penalty. But Barr, rather than replacing the ball where it was, hit it onto the green. That's a two-shot penalty.

Witnessing this entire scene was Tucker. He hurried over to Barr and told him he shouldn't finish the hole, that it might cost him a disqualification.

Tucker then asked for a rules inquiry. That inquiry verified the three-shot penalty.

Houston Coach Dave Williams was upset after hearing of the penalty, but said little until the Rules Committee had officially reaffirmed it after Barr had finished his round. What followed was a scene rarely displayed in the gentlemen's game of golf.

Williams demanded to see Rod Myers, president of the NCAA Rules Committee. He angrily blamed the penalty on Tucker and then launched into a diatribe, as reported by the Lodi *News-Sentinel*: "I want to know what can be done tomorrow to keep Karl Tucker from waving his hands all over the place while my boys are trying to putt. Because if nothing is going to be done, I'll be out there tomorrow."

Tucker stepped in and said, "I'm here to defend myself." A Rules Committee official moved between them and cautioned, "Gentlemen, what are we doing in public? Let's go inside."

But Williams brushed him away. "Naw, I'll be out there tomorrow. There's going to be some penalties. We're going to have plenty!"

As Williams and his team stalked away, Barr tried to calm his angry coach, saying, according to Mike Sorensen's *Deseret News* account, "Coach, it was a legitimate rule. There's no need to get upset about it." (And Barr later admitted: "It was my mistake and a good ruling. I appreciated Coach Tucker for pointing out the rule violation.")

A flabbergasted Tucker stood there, not quite believing what he had just heard. The coach had probably saved Barr from disqualification and Houston from having to count another player's 82 (Barr shot 72 with the penalty), which would have instantly taken them out of the race!

Williams and Tucker, good friends over many years, made up the following morning, allowing attention to shift back to the interesting three-team race for the NCAA title that was about to begin.

The honor of "anchorman," or last golfer on the course for BYU, went to Dick Zokol because of his team-leading score. In him the team found a willing standard-bearer. "I was very proud to do it," says Zokol. "I felt I owed a lot to my teammates and BYU. I wanted to bring it on home." Indeed, in a close tournament, the "anchorman" might be called on to bring it home on a pressure-packed 18th hole.

The three-team race soon dropped to two. BYU and Oral Roberts were holding their own, but Houston had fallen back far enough to not pose a serious threat.

As the golfers played on, hole after hole, they had little idea how the tournament was progressing. They could only match their own scores with those of opposing golfers playing with them. Imagine the tension! Five golfers are playing simultaneously on different holes, so team scores are changing constantly. A three-stroke lead can be gone in five minutes in a round that can last more than four hours. Even a team's coach must scramble around the course to stay up-to-date. A player's most frequent source of information is a "hot tip," in reality little more than a rumor, from the gallery.

So the players did not know that they were locked in one of the classic two-team races in NCAA tournament history. The lead changed hands several times during the round, though neither could ever manage more than a two-shot advantage.

And that tension! After Dave DeSantis had triple-bogeyed hole No. 4, he was afraid he had blown it for

the team. He resolved to play steady golf over the
final 14 holes, hoping his lapse wouldn't come back
to haunt BYU.

And Zokol, after double-bogeying No. 14, looked
up and shrugged at Tucker. "If you think you're
going to get me to frown," the coach replied to the
body English, "you're wrong." But Zokol could also
afford a gesture of relief: His Oral Roberts playing
partner, Joe Rassett, had also double-bogeyed the
hole!

Zokol regrouped with an important birdie on the
next hole. And up ahead some of his teammates
were completing their rounds with some big pressure shots. Willardson was the first to finish.
Though he had not played particularly well all week,
he parred the final hole, giving the Cougars a one-
shot lead. DeSantis followed with another par, and
while his 76 would end up as BYU's non-counting
score, matched against ORU's Jim Wilson's 80 it
gave the Cougars the team title in case the tourney
ended in a tie. That was as good as gaining another
stroke.

Clearwater was the next finishing golfer, and he
wasn't too happy about landing his second shot in a
sand trap not too far from the hole. But ORU's Jim
Kane had just played his fourth shot on the par-4
hole and still faced a 15-foot putt for a bogey.

So the BYU golfer, relieved that he could still pick
up at least one more shot for his team, lofted a sand
shot that landed on the green like a feather and
settled just four feet from the hole. After Kane connected with a clutch putt to keep his misery to a
bogey, Clearwater found the edge of the cup to get
his par and finish with a solid final-round 70. BYU
led by two, plus the tiebreaker, with just two golfers
still to play.

One of those golfers was Fehr—the freshman.

Could he stand the pressure? His drive off the tee answered that question; it landed beautifully in the fairway. Oral Roberts' Bryan Norton, a senior, sprayed his tee shot far into the right-hand rough. Fehr hit his second shot easily onto the green, about 25 feet from the hole. Norton couldn't shake the rough with two more strokes, then he knocked the ball into a trap at the back of the green. Even with a superb sand shot that came close to going into the hole, Norton was tagged with a double-bogey.

It took Fehr three putts to finish his round, a 72, but the Cougars still had a three-shot lead with just one golfer, anchorman Zokol, to go.

The four Cougars who had finished their rounds knew that. But Zokol, who had just smacked a nice drive off the 18th tee, was still in the dark. "I thought we were even," insists Zokol, who was paired with Rassett of Oral Roberts. "I thought we had a two-man duel on our hands."

Over the past few holes, Zokol had been pleading with Tucker to let him know how the team was faring. Tucker refused, but then added he'd tell him after his tee shot on 18.

Former BYU player Tom Costello was the first to Zokol with the news: "Unless you break your leg, we've got it!" He assured Costello he could, indeed, live with a three-shot lead.

Zokol decided now was no time to take chances. He aimed for the "fat" part of the green, then knocked the ball into the left rear bunker, a long way from the pin and the championship.

As he started to walk down the fairway, Zokol almost seemed to hobble—sort of like he had a broken leg.

Willardson's televised appeal to Zokol's sand shot must have had its effect. The ball was flying cleanly out of the trap and over the rough. It sailed briskly toward the flag, then lighted on the green.

And it *did* bite! Had it not, it might have rolled clear off the lower side of the green. Instead, it spun to a stop, some 15 feet from the title. Willardson let out a restrained little whoop to show his pleasure at the ball's obedience.

That did it. Unless Zokol literally broke his leg or was struck by lightning, the title was BYU's. And there wasn't a dark cloud in sight.

The anchorman conservatively "brought it on home" in a pair of shots, nailing down the final two-stroke victory.

The Cougars went wild . . . that is, as wild as dignified golfers dared. They trotted, not sprinted, toward the green and sort of tiptoed across it. The team wanted to celebrate, but not have to replace any divots afterwards.

It was about as civilized a celebration for a national championship as you'll ever see. But to a man, inner emotions raged. Tears flowed freely and the eyes could not conceal how much this meant.

Especially to Tucker. Normally ebullient under any circumstances, he was momentarily left without words—understandable words, that is. The players had done it for him, they told him . . .

And for Joanne, whose ailment had not allowed her to be here. "We've got to call her," said the coach, and suddenly he was his old self again. He was like a little boy in anticipation of her reaction to his first NCAA championship.

Duke Coach Rod Myers, at the trophy presentation, said: "A lot of us thought when Bobby Clampett turned pro, there went BYU. We were wrong." They *were* wrong. Because behind Clampett was a highly balanced team strong enough to bring BYU its first outright NCAA championship of any kind, one that probably meant a whole lot more to these golfers because Clampett *wasn't* there.

Tucker later added this praise, something he still believes: "I've had teams with more talented players, but I've never, *never* had a better team."

A rousing celebration, complete with non-alcoholic champagne, awaited the BYU "family" that evening. A very satisfying return trip to Provo followed.

And the dwarfs (who were never called that again), and their NCAA trophies, lived happily ever after . . .

4

The Drought Ends

Something was wrong at Eddie Kimball's Saturday evening party to celebrate that day's victory over Utah. The BYU football coach saw that his dozen-or-so guests had plenty to eat, drink and talk about. But something was still amiss.

There was no victory to celebrate. But then, on the other hand, there was no loss to lament. In fact, the guests at Kimball's party didn't even know the score of that afternoon's BYU-Utah contest!

The 750-mile gulf that separated Coach Kimball from the BYU campus seemed like 7,500 miles. He lifted the phone to try another call to Utah, to find someone—anyone—who knew how his team had done. A collective moan rose from the anxious group. Still no long distance lines available.

Whoa! Stop right there. What on earth is the coach of the Brigham Young University football team doing 750 miles away on the day of his team's biggest game? And how is it he doesn't even know who won it?

Read on, dear reader, read on.

Eddie Kimball's world, like so many others in October 1942, had been tipped upside down. The shame of Pearl Harbor, only 10 months removed, still smoldered in the national consciousness. The winds of war that loomed over the horizon for several years had begun to sweep across the United States at gale force. It picked up young men by the thousands and whisked them away to the Pacific, Europe and Africa.

One such gust picked up Kimball, who left behind a wife, young children and the BYU football team he had coached for five years. He was told his job would be waiting after completing his duties with the Navy in the Pacific. Until then, his squad would just have to manage — somehow.

And lest you think BYU fans stayed awake at night, fretting over this disturbing development, try to imagine yourself living in the world of 1942. Your daily newspaper doesn't just relate such bothersome developments as an increased federal deficit, higher inflation or a war in faraway Iraq. It chronicles events that may permanently change the course of the world. It tells of a powerful Nazi dictator whose forces have spread through Europe like a brushfire and conquered the charred remains of several countries. It trumpets the successes of a Japanese government ruthlessly bent on expansion of its power in the Pacific. It recounts battles where hundreds, maybe thousands, of American lives are lost — perhaps a son, brother, cousin or boyfriend among them.

So while the BYU football team prepared for a long, trying spell without its coach, the city of Stalingrad was clinging to a life almost squeezed out of it by a German siege. Americans were feeling the effects of the huge war effort through rationing of many taken-for-granted household basics. And the Japanese had landed on Guadalcanal.

Football (and other sports) assumed its natural and proper role in such a world—a pleasant diversion on a Saturday afternoon, something to take a little of the sting out of a cruel, cruel world.

Just how topsy-turvy was the world of early October 1942?

At the same time Gary Cooper, as ex-Yankee great Lou Gehrig, was filling hankies with tears in theatres across the United States in the movie *Pride of the Yankees,* his equally proud New York baseball descendants were being swept four games to none in the World Series by the upstart St. Louis Cardinals. More than 68,000 people sat in shocked silence in hallowed Yankee Stadium as the Cards, led by young Stan Musial and Enos Slaughter, proceeded to dismantle Joe DiMaggio and the Yankee powerhouse.

Was nothing safe anymore?

While the world changed around them, Utahns had something they could bank on. It was true before the Depression, true during the Depression and true in the years leading to World War II. Simply stated, it was that the University of Utah never lost to BYU in football. Never. Ever.

BYU began playing football around the turn of the century, but a fatality during a game caused the school to drop the sport for more than a decade. As far as the university is concerned, its official football history began when it was next played—1922.

From 1922 through 1941, BYU's record against Utah was three ties and 17 losses. No wins. In those 20 games the Utes shut out the Cougars 11 times, compiled an average score of 25-3 and outpointed them by a total of 490-65.

BYU scored two touchdowns against the Utes on just a pair of occasions—little consolation in games lost 45-13 and 35-13. The rest of the time, it was a single touchdown or nothing.

And, oh yes, the Utes managed to paint BYU's cougar red more than the Cougars could redecorate the block "U" with blue paint.

That's the amazing thing. As lopsided as this rivalry was, students and players from the two schools remained just that—rivals. And they treated each other as good rivals ought to. There was always spirited, intense play on the field or court; occasional overindulgences after the game; and a long list of legendary, but well-documented pranks, some of epic magnitude.

Most of this was good, clean fun, of course. Our parents and grandparents weren't hoodlums. They did, however, live in a different era from ours.

The universities themselves were hardly today's burgeoning mini-cities of 25,000-plus students. Utah reported 4,200 students in 1942; BYU had about 1,000 fewer, or about as many as today's large high schools.

BYU students were admiring the just-completed, modern Joseph Smith Building, the final step in transferring the majority of student activity from lower campus, along University Avenue, to a large hill just east of the aging buildings. And if you climbed to the top of that hill and looked south, you wouldn't see endless rows of houses and student apartment complexes. You'd see endless rows of corn, alfalfa or other crops growing beside scattered farmhouses and silos.

Football was played on a field now buried by BYU's physical education building. Up to 12,000 people (though games typically drew less than half that number) could watch the game from bleachers that covered the steep hillside to the east of the field.

And the game those people came to see was not at all similar to the flashy spectacle that now draws 65,000 fans to Provo. Most teams, including BYU and Utah, ran from the single wing formation, a plodding, run-oriented offense that usually gobbled up only three- and four-yard chunks at a time. Passing was viewed as the second-best way to move the ball, and its use was infrequent, particularly behind one's own 50-yard line.

Unlike the 275-pound behemoths of today, the average lineman of 1942 weighed 195 pounds. And while he wore padding, it was not nearly as extensive or effective as the armor of today. Heads were covered by simple leather helmets that offered no protection to the face. Most team members played offense and defense, something unheard of in this age of specialization. Injuries were not treated with today's scientific skill. Minor maladies often became major (and then lifelong) ones because of lack of treatment. Then, as now, players were accustomed to "playing hurt."

Field position was just as important a weapon as the forward pass. Being stuck on your own 5-yard line was akin to standing at the very edge of a precipice. The quick kick, a surprise punt often employed on third down and long yardage situations, was used by some teams as often as the pass. A wise strategy was to maintain good field position with as conservative an offense as the defense would allow, then take advantage of blocked kicks or turnovers in the opponent's territory. A big-gaining play or long drive was just icing on the cake—they just didn't happen that often.

If football teams had to work harder for their points, their players also were forced to work harder off the field. Scholarships weren't as common (and often included just tuition and books), and most players had to find a job to meet living expenses (even while playing football). These jobs didn't involve making sure the automatic sprinklers came on. They were often physically taxing, as with one player who scrubbed ceilings and shoveled coal— after football practice.

They were simpler days in many ways, to be sure. Long-maintained college traditions were still adhered to. Imagine a BYU campus where freshmen were forced to shine shoes, sing at odd moments, carry an upperclassman's books or remain silent until spoken to.

That was college life in 1942. And part of that cherished tradition involved choosing another school as a rival and doing all the things rivals are supposed to do to each other.

So every year the BYU team and students, with gusto, would point to the Utah game, still the state's top attraction of the season, and vow, "This'll be the year." And every year the Utes would, with obvious glee, send them back to Provo, vow unfulfilled.

As you might suspect, the words *hex* and *jinx* began to pop up frequently. And for good reason, perhaps. BYU did not have that *bad* a football program. In the 20 years since 1922, the school had produced eight winning teams and four that won as many as they lost. That means just eight of BYU's 20 teams had suffered through a losing season (including five of the first six).

While the Cougars didn't exactly shake the Wasatch Mountains against Utah State (then Utah State Agricultural College), either, they had beaten or tied the Aggies nine times in 20 years. Their 54-0 whipping of USAC in 1937 still stands as one of BYU's ten biggest winning margins ever (and the only rout on that list before 1967).

But playing the Utes was something else. In BYU's great 8-1 campaign of 1932, Utah routed the Cougars 29-0. In the remaining eight games, the Y allowed but 21 points. In the two-loss seasons of '30 and '39, Utah again smashed the Cougars 34-7 and 35-13.

If BYU wasn't bad, then Utah must have been awesome. Indeed, Ute teams of the '30s and early '40s were deep in talent and well-financed. BYU, while frequently blessed with considerable individual talent, could never match Utah's bench strength, or its pocketbook. (How ironic that Utah now points to these same two factors as reasons for BYU's recent domination of the series!) The legendary Ike Armstrong had established an enviable dynasty in Salt Lake City, one that produced winner after winner. Ike was a great coach. He taught fundamentals well. He knew how to recruit and motivate players. And he knew what it took to beat BYU. Would it really require much more, though, than standing in front of a team in the locker room and asking: "How would you like to be known as the first team to lose to BYU in 20 years? How would you like to live with *that* the rest of your lives?"

Ike was also used to calling his own shots. One of them was refusing to play BYU in Provo. Year in and year out, if the Cougars wanted to have the Utes on their schedule, the game had to be played in Salt Lake. The most frequently mentioned reason was finances — that Utah could draw more to its games than BYU. But many people thought something else was involved, as well: Ike simply wanted it that way.

But competition was getting tougher for Ike and his Utes. Diminutive Eddie Kimball was quietly building the foundation of an excellent program 50 miles to the south. A noted football tactician in his own right, Kimball had four winning seasons and a record of 21-15-7 in his first five years at BYU.

A few stories will illustrate why he is still spoken of with greatest respect by his players, though now in their 60s:

Jim Hecker met Kimball at a Chicago college all-star practice he managed to sneak into. The native of Fond du Lac, Wisconsin, was so impressed with Kimball that he showed up, unannounced, for the first day of school, and, of course, to play football.

Herman Longhurst, a promising high school prospect from Pocatello, Idaho, called Kimball one day. He wondered if two of his football-playing friends, originally destined for University of Idaho scholarships but now disenchanted with the school, could come along with him to play at BYU. Kimball drove to Pocatello, brought the three to Provo, helped them register for school and put them up in his own home for several days.

Kimball's stature and generosity had landed him Hecker, Longhurst, and Longhurst's friends, Bob Orr and Mike Mills — all starters on the 1942 team.

And his efforts began paying dividends on the field. Only once did he lose badly to Utah in five years. His teams brought back two of the three ties BYU had ever managed against the Utes.

When World War II whisked away head coach Eddie Kimball and assistant Wayne Soffe (above center and right), Floyd Millet (above left) took over — the entire BYU athletic program. Millet's task was made easier by athletes like team captain Herman Longhurst (right), a "triple threat" tailback.

"Lining up" in 1942 often meant for military service, too.

Halfback Bob Orr sweeps around left end during the BYU-Utah game.

If Utah's Armstrong felt the Cougars finally closing in on him, it was for good reason. BYU's current
crop of seniors had suffered a 35-13 rout as freshmen, then closed to within 12-6 as sophomores. As
juniors they inched ever closer. A 90-yard Longhurst interception return set up an early BYU touchdown. Were it not for saving tackle on another 67-
yard Longhurst run, or a mid-fourth quarter drive,
Utah would not have escaped with a fortunate 6-6
tie.

So it was with unmatched enthusiasm that Kimball's squad gathered for practice sessions that
spring of 1942. This senior-rich team's cry of "this'll
be the year," no longer sounded hollow and mean-
ingless in Salt Lake City. Nor did Wisconsin walk-on
Hecker's brash public prediction that the Cougars
would win the next game with Utah—by a touchdown.

But the hope of spring quickly faded into the
reality of summer. That June war gust carried away
the leader and chief architect of this optimistic and
hungry BYU team. Eddie Kimball was off to war.

Assistant coach Floyd Millet was in the middle of
a long recruiting trip to Arizona and New Mexico
when his boss joined the Navy. Incredibly, he knew
nothing about Kimball's plans until he returned to
Provo. "I was as surprised as anyone," he recalls.

Millet wasn't so surprised when BYU President
Franklin Harris asked him to take over the football
program, and also become the school's athletic director, until Kimball returned. The team's only other
assistant coach, Wayne Soffe, was also bound for the
Navy.

Adding these positions to his existing ones as
head basketball and track coach would make Millet

a busy, busy man. But he also knew the school had nowhere else to turn, so he accepted. He'd hold down the fort while his colleagues were away.

BYU's lack of choices didn't mean it was inheriting a lightweight substitute. Millet had proven himself an able assistant to the popular Kimball the previous five seasons. His first BYU basketball team, in 1941-42, lost just three games and was ranked No. 12 in the nation. His 1942-43 team was invited to play in the prestigious Madison Square Garden preseason doubleheader in New York, an annual event matching two New York City teams with invited guests from elsewhere in the country. The Cougars were the first Utah team to ever play in the world-famous arena.

Millet seemed to possess all the qualities of a successful coach. "He is good-looking, capable and well-liked by the men he coaches," describes the 1942 *Banyan*, BYU's yearbook. "A hard worker, Millet very seldom lets the players go before the sun is setting, unless it's the day before a game . . ." Demanding that hard work was an intense competitive spirit, one Millet's friends insist still shines through, even in friendly games of basketball or racquetball.

A native of Mesa, Arizona, the new head coach attended LDS Church-operated Gila Junior College in Thatcher, about 125 miles to the east. His coach there, Golden Romney, talked Millet into attending BYU. There he earned letters in football, basketball and track and all-conference honors in football and basketball.

Millet graduated from BYU in 1934, during the depth of the Depression. "I was extremely lucky to get a coaching job at Davis High School," he says. He directed the basketball, baseball and track programs at the Farmington, Utah, school and assisted in football. He was hired by BYU three years later to help new football coach Eddie Kimball and head up the track program.

Millet first got his taste of BYU futility against Utah in 29-0, 21-6 and 43-0 thumpings the three years he played for the Cougars. He was a fullback, "the man in motion," in BYU's innovative T-formation offense. G. Ott Romney, a coach Millet says "was 20 years ahead of his time," was one of only a handful of coaches in the nation to use the revolutionary new scheme. And though the "T" may have helped BYU teams compile a respectable 17-10 record during Millet's three years as a player, it didn't help them conquer Utah.

Things didn't change much during Millet's three-year tenure at Davis High, in the heart of Ute country, or in his five years as an assistant football coach at BYU.

"It (losing to Utah) was really getting monotonous," Millet says. He decided enough was enough. Not long after being asked to fill in for Kimball, he sat down to plot team goals for the 1942 season. With World War II rapidly closing in, Millet knew the team might not even be able to complete its season, or might be seriously depleted by year's-end. So the goal at the top of his list wasn't necessarily to win the Mountain States Conference championship or to even compile a winning record. His No. 1 objective for the 1942 season:

Beat Utah.

Such an objective sounds incredibly simple-minded in an era when 10-victory seasons and romps over Utah are commonplace. But it was a bold goal in 1942, one that would mean as much to the athletic program and the people of Utah Valley as a first conference championship or another winning season. And it would probably be just as difficult to obtain.

Millet began chasing his goal with an intensity fitting his competitive nature. Convincing his players to accept the challenge was the easy part. The seniors of 1942, particularly, knew two things long before Millet gathered them for fall practice: They were coming very close to victory over Utah — and the war. It didn't take much, then, for Millet to persuade his players. Beating Utah would be a great final "fling" before inevitable war duty.

The coach worked his team extra hard in fall practices. He felt the key to overcoming Utah's superior manpower and depth was a squad conditioned to play well the entire 60 minutes, if necessary. Workouts were often tedious repetitions of such basic skills as tackling and open-field blocking. Millet knew the fewer errors, even simple errors, his team made, the greater its chances for victory.

But Millet's final tactic may have had the most impact. While his team wouldn't be able to dominate Utah physically, he conceded, it certainly could mentally. He began what he termed a "psychological warfare" campaign.

"I put together a list of Utah players and began gathering information on each of them," Millet said. "Most of the players were already well known to our team members. I pointed out that they really weren't invincible, either as individuals or as a group."

And though he may not have realized it, Millet fired another salvo in the psychological war when he hired Paul Rose as his assistant coach. Rose had coached at Murray High School in the Salt Lake Valley after a successful collegiate career at — horrors! — the University of Utah.

If BYU fans had some reservations about Millet, who previously coached at a school that sent athlete after athlete to Utah, what must their feelings have been about Rose, who actually played there?

The new assistant coach, who would be in charge of the linemen, assured everyone that "your allegiance is with the group you're with." He quickly became a valued ally to Millet in his mission. Rose brought a different perspective to practice sessions. He had played for Ike Armstrong (against Millet, in fact). He was familiar with the successful Ute system. He knew what confidence could do for a team.

So when Rose also began telling the players they really *could* beat Utah, it only reinforced and cemented what Millet had been asserting all along. How could the players not believe it, coming from an ex-Ute himself?

The war on the mind continued every day during the fall. Sometime between all the tackling and blocking and running and sweating, Millet and Rose would call their players together and remind them about Utah — either a tendency a particular player had or something the Utes did as a team that they should watch for. And always there was that assurance: "We'll beat 'em!"

When those same three words started showing up in area newspapers, more than the BYU football team sat up in alarm. Such bold public predictions were far from in style in 1942. Millet added he didn't mean to sound brash; he just wanted to show his team how much confidence he had in them.

But the psychological warfare couldn't change one fact: Utah was just one of nine opponents on BYU's schedule, and the team would have to play

Montana State and Wyoming before getting its shot at the Utes.

The Cougars' 12-6 non-league win at Bozeman, Montana, was an encouraging start. Montana State had thumped BYU 20-7 the year before, and the victory, on the road, over the solid Bobcats was a good way to begin the season.

But the 13-6 home loss that followed to Wyoming, and not one of its better teams, was just as disheartening. The Cowboys battered BYU with both turnovers and injuries. A bruising defense, 46-yard screen pass and 79-yard drive early in the second half was all it took for the visitors to return to Laramie winners.

Several Cougars were left hobbling. But the most serious casualty was to BYU's confidence. Sometime in the coming week it would have to recover sufficiently to suit up for the Utah game.

Floyd Millet worked his injury-riddled squad long and hard the Monday after the Wyoming disappointment. He drilled his players on blocking and tackling, skills he felt were missing against the Cowboys. He also drilled them on Utah again, reminding them that the loss to Wyoming shouldn't have anything to do with their upcoming performance against the Utes.

Millet had some new psychological ammunition as well. Utah had lost on Saturday to Arizona, 14-0, its second straight shutout loss. Granted, Arizona and first-week foe Santa Clara (a West Coast power then) were far better teams than BYU opponents Montana State and Wyoming. But the Utes had lost, and looked bad in doing so. The Utah offense, which was so anemic against Arizona, helped make the

Wildcats the top-rated defense in the nation that week. In fact, Ike Armstrong was so disgusted with his team's play that he ordered a workout in the fieldhouse immediately after arrival from Tucson, Arizona — at nine-thirty Monday night!

By Tuesday it was apparent that injuries and recoveries would play a key factor in Saturday's game. BYU's problems were centered in the line. Guard Robert Hull was nursing three cracked ribs. Another guard, Fielding Abbott, had a banged-up knee. But the biggest blow was seeing the two stand-out tackles, Dee Call (hip pointer) and Ken Bird (ankle), sidelined. Though the Cougars had other capable linemen, including all-conference center Reed Nilsen and all-star end Mike Mills, they weren't given much of a chance to beat the Utes without Bird and Call. Good tackles were almost as essential to an effective single-wing offense as wide receivers are to BYU's passing attack today. They were the players most responsible for opening holes at the point of attack for ballcarriers.

(In the single wing, the quarterback lined up behind and to the side of center. He called the plays and signals, but did not take the snap. He was primarily a blocking back. The tailback was placed several paces behind the center and took the snap most of the time. The fullback was at the tailback's side and also took occasional snaps. "To put together an effective single wing," said Millet, "you needed to start with a triple-threat tailback — one who could run, pass and kick — a good blocking quarterback . . . and great tackles.")

Having both Bird and Call out with injuries would be especially devastating to BYU's offense.

Utah's injuries were primarily to backfield personnel, but Ike Armstrong had plenty of capable athletes to fill in. It was just a matter of *where* they'd play. Star tailback Wally Kelly and quarterback Chet Kim were healthy. But wingback Billy Han of Honolulu injured an ankle in practice Tuesday, then found out hours later by cable his mother had died. And fullback Woody Peterson was gradually gaining strength after an injury that kept him from playing against Arizona. He was expected to be ready by Saturday.

BYU's backfield, meanwhile, appeared to be in top shape. Quarterbacks Glen Oliverson and Mark Weed; fullbacks Marcel Chatterton and Fred Whitney; and halfbacks Jim Hecker, Bob Orr and Herman Longhurst were all expected to be injury-free for the Utah game. "Slippery-hipped" Longhurst, as he was often called, was the team's "triple-threat" player and captain. It was an experienced, talented backfield, one felt to be distinctly better than the Utes'.

By Thursday, BYU's fortunes took a dramatic turn for the better. Both Bird and Call were back at practice and ready to give it a try. Their status was still questionable for the game, but their very presence at practice seemed to lift the team's spirit. Millet continued to drill the squad on blocking, tackling and "psychological warfare."

Ike Armstrong, meanwhile, continued to juggle his backfield, trying to find the most effective combination to oppose BYU. He worked the Utes overtime in practices all week, primarily on pass defense, a weakness he was afraid BYU might be able to exploit.

Utah newspapers began warming to the fact that something unique in the history of the rivalry was unfolding. The word probable began replacing the word possible when describing BYU's prospects for victory. United Press International's Leo H. Petersen predicted a Utah victory ("too much tradition," he wrote), but most other sports writers and observers in the state saw the game as a toss-up, or even installed BYU as a slight favorite. "With the caliber of teams at Provo," wrote Salt Lake *Tribune* Sports Editor Jimmy Hodgson, "the 'jinx' is bound to end sooner or later."

Eddie Kimball planned to spring a little surprise on his football team. The absentee coach had managed to get permission from his commanding officer to fly from San Diego, where he was training, to Salt Lake City so he could watch the BYU-Utah game. He even had an airplane lined up to transport him there. Kimball anxiously counted down the days until he could be with his boys again, even if only briefly.

But just three days before the game, he received new orders and was told to report immediately to his new commander. Knowing that asking for time off to see a football game 750 miles away wouldn't be the best way to start a relationship with a new superior, Kimball decided to cancel the trip.

To help ease the pain of not being in Salt Lake City for the big game, the coach asked some BYU acquaintances to come to his quarters for a Saturday night "victory party."

Anyone who has devoted a great deal of time to prepare for a single event can appreciate the mixed feelings of Millet, Rose and their BYU players as the start of the game neared. There's excitement, intensity and anticipation. But there's also a deep, gnawing nervousness that grabs at the stomach, often quietly. What if the event doesn't live up to my high expectations? What if I don't do as well as I'm supposed to? What if I fail? It's a little like death, where distant anticipation is much different from the cold, impending, fast-closing reality.

Everything was set. A beautiful, brisk autumn afternoon was the setting. More than 10,000 people, including some 2,500 BYU boosters, would be the witnesses. A talented University of Utah team would be the foil.

BYU's confidence was about to be put to the test. The campaign to prepare the team mentally for the game would now have to be matched with physical skills to accomplish a clear-cut goal. In the fierce battle of bodies and wills about to take place, would the Cougars have enough to finally carry them over the top?

Whatever uncertainty lay below the jerseys and pads of the BYU team about to take the field was well hidden by excitement. It was one of those rare occasions, Millet recalls, that he had to calm a team down in a pregame talk. He, like his players, couldn't wait for the game to start.

Neither team showed much more than nervousness for most of the first quarter. Dee Call recovered a fumble on the Utes' first play from scrimmage on the BYU 48-yard line. The Cougars couldn't move the ball and punted. Utah turned it over again a few plays later, this time on their own 29. The Cougars had been given a great chance to score, but couldn't progress more than five yards. On fourth and seven from the 26, an incompleted pass ended the brief threat. Today, a field goal attempt from that spot would give the Cougars three points more than half the time. But the kicking game was far less reliable. The disdained pass was even preferred to attempting a kick as a fourth-down option. The score remained 0-0.

The teams traded possessions again without offensive flashes of brilliance, save for Herman Long-hurst's 15-yard burst. (Bob Orr's 11-yard run was canceled by BYU's third offsides penalty of the quarter.) Utah, operating from its own 15-yard line, shocked everyone by calling a pass. It gained 18 yards. But a fumble on the next play had BYU set up again, this time on the Utah 40.

Orr's nine-yard run (no offsides) to the Utah 31 ended a first quarter dominated by Utah's turnovers and BYU's penalties and offensive staleness. Classic rivals may have been playing, but it was hardly a classic game so far.

The single yard gained by fullback Marcel Chatterton to open the second quarter sent out a new signal, though. It was a tough-to-come-by yard that gave BYU its first first down while approaching the Utes' goal. An offsides penalty (virtually the only infraction called on either team all game) on Utah moved the ball to the 25. Orr's second-down run gave the Cougars another first down at the 20. Fred Whitney, a hard-running fullback, powered for nine yards to the Utah 8 for still another first down.

Hey, this was an honest-to-goodness drive! But it wasn't being accomplished with the pass, the anticipated strategy against Utah, but rather the run, which Utah was adept at defending. (Millet explains his surprising game strategy—to run rather than pass—this way: "If I was going to beat Utah, I wanted to do it at their own game." What was that? "Run right over the top of you.")

Orr ran right over the top of the Utes for five yards on the first two downs, setting up third and goal from the 3. Whitney could only drive to the 2 on the next play. Fourth and goal from the 2. Would BYU go for a safe three points or risk it all for the potential six? Remembering that this is the same coach who said he wanted to beat the Utes by running right over them, is there any doubt what Millet's decision would be? Whitney took the handoff and crashed through the Ute defense for a touchdown. The extra point wasn't close. (Maybe that also explains why Millet wanted to go for the TD on fourth down!) BYU still led 6-0 early in the second quarter.

Utah, deciding they had fumbled the ball enough, went to the air. After picking up 10 yards on the first pass play, they lost the next to Cougar Reed Nilsen's interception at the BYU 48. The center-linebacker was leading his team to a sterling defensive effort thus far. Of Utah's first five possessions, four had ended with turnovers.

But if BYU was Superman on defense, it was something much more mortal on offense. While untouched by turnovers, BYU took an offsides penalty, halting a drive that barely crossed the 50. Field position, though, began working for the Cougars, for after stopping the Utes without a first down, they took possession of the ball at the Utah 45. With a drive slightly longer than the scoring 40-yard effort earlier in the quarter, the Cougars could take an impressive two-touchdown lead into the locker room at halftime. Whitney started the drive well with two runs totaling 10 yards. With a first and 10 on the 35, though, a BYU drive bogged down again. Orr punted from the 41 on fourth down. The ball was downed at the 6-inch line!

A first-down quick kick attempt by the Utes was partially blocked and rolled only to the 27. Now the Cougars had an even better chance to grab the big lead. Longhurst ran a single yard on first down, then threw an interception on the next play.

BYU would still have one more scoring opportunity before halftime. Longhurst redeemed himself for the interception by taking off on a dazzling 40-yard run to the Utah 20 with 1:15 remaining. But, you guessed it — offsides, this time on both the Utes and the Cougars. However, the offsetting foul was good enough to call back the play.

The half ended with BYU leading 6-0 and totally dominating play. But the Cougars were frustrated with all the missed chances that could have made the score much more convincing. They outrushed the Utes 87-22 and outgained them 92-49 in total yardage. They had caused four turnovers and never allowed the Utah offense to cross the 50-yard line. Yet their lead could still be wiped out with only one play, any play, and one kick.

After seeing 10- and 16-yard runs by Jim Hecker nullified by offsides calls to open the third quarter, the Cougars saw just how quickly their total domination could be canceled. A third-down quick kick was blocked and recovered on the BYU 21-yard line. U fullback Woody Peterson rumbled for nine yards. Tailback Wally Kelly hit quarterback Chet Kim with a pass covering another nine yards. And Peterson took care of the final three yards. One play. One kick. Utah led 7-6. Utah's four errors in its own territory had resulted in just one BYU touchdown. And now the Cougars' first mistake in their own end cost them dearly.

If BYU felt the need to reassert control of the game, they certainly picked an unusual way to do it. After seeing his team gain nine yards on its next three offensive plays, Millet instructed them to go for it on fourth and one — from their own 29-yard line!

The Cougars made it, but this derring-do was quickly forgotten when the drive was halted after the next three plays. BYU punted to the Utah 27, and the Utes returned the favor with a second-down quick kick that sailed all the way to the Cougar 7.

The Y's offense failed to move the ball, and was faced with a frightening third and long from the shadow of its own goal line. The quick kick sailed high and long to the Utah 45, where the U's swift Kelly took it and raced down the sideline all the way to the BYU 20.

All of a sudden, the Cougars' domination had ended and they were fighting just to stay in the game. Kelly tried the same sideline and gained 12 yards to the 8. First and goal Utah. But an offsides infraction against the Redskins seemed to give BYU's defense back the toughness it had temporarily lost. Kelly was stopped for no gain; Billy Han was piled up for a three-yard loss; and Kelly was sacked back at the 30 by Bird and Nilsen. The Utes punted into the end zone on fourth down.

BYU couldn't move the ball again next series, but that didn't erase the sense of relief they felt at having survived the third quarter still, relatively, intact. BYU trailed 7-6, but now saw Utah starting from its own 31. The ever-crucial field position battle had at least temporarily been neutralized.

The Utes gained but four yards on the next three plays and were forced to punt. As the fans sat back to watch still another kick arch gracefully into a resplendent autumn sky, they instead saw it — blocked! Dee Call had burst in from his right tackle spot and cleanly blocked the kick, so cleanly that it rolled clear back to the Utah 10-yard line. Just when momentum had seemed to shift away from the Cougars, here was the break they'd been waiting for.

First and goal just inside the 10-yard line. It didn't matter now that BYU was just 1-for-4 in converting Utah-territory errors. But it sure would matter if that was soon 1-for-5!

Longhurst found no room in the Ute line on first down. Whitney powered his way to the 6 on second. Longhurst's run off tackle carried him only to the 3 on third down. Fourth and goal from the 3? Again, need you ask when Millet was willing to try a fourth down play on his own 29? Longhurst took the snap and started to head around right end. Good blocks from Call and Mike Mills, the duo that had just given the Cougars this chance, allowed the tailback to go wide and sprint for the end zone. He crossed the goal line well ahead of his Redskin pursuers. BYU may have missed scoring opportunities, but it was now 3-for-3 on clutch fourth down plays, two of which brought touchdowns!

BYU led 12-7 after the extra-point attempt again went awry. The Utes wouldn't even need to convert a PAT to win the game, just cross the goal line one more time. And there was plenty of time left.

A third-down quick kick near midfield again caught the Cougars off guard. It rolled dead at the BYU 9-yard line. The Cougars' own third-down quick kick was partially blocked. The Utes now had a first down on BYU's 32-yard line, an excellent position to move from for the winning score. BYU's defense had apparently stopped Utah again, when on third down Wayne Page took the ball on an end around and carried it 19 yards to the 10. It would be the Utes' longest gainer of the day.

BYU was shocked, but had to regroup quickly, for Utah was approaching the ball for a new series of downs they were sure would win the ball game. Fullback Peterson tried the middle for no gain. Kelly went off tackle for just two yards. Peterson managed just two more on third down. The Cougar defense had held up again under pressure, but now came the real test. Fourth and goal from the 6. The Utes had to go for the touchdown. What would they do?

It didn't take BYU's Bird long to recognize the end around to Page unfolding again. And while he had been fooled last time, he didn't want it to happen again. He pursued Page and dropped him on the 5-yard line, far short of his, and the Utes', goal.

Time was winding down now, and the Cougars wanted to use as much of it as they could. Three running plays gained just two yards, but also a large chunk of the clock. A dangerous fourth-down punt still had to be executed from the goal line. An earlier blocked kick had cost the Utes a touchdown. A block here would almost assuredly hand Utah a dramatic, last-minute win. The snap was back. Orr quickly stepped into the ball and punted it high over the out-stretched arms of the onrushing Utes.

Utah had the ball on BYU's 43 for a last desperate shot at a winning touchdown. Kelly gained just three yards on a first-down run. Time out. Then a pass was caught by Utah at about the 25-yard line . . . bobbled . . . then picked off in midair by Longhurst. When the clock was again started, BYU didn't even need to put the ball in play! The game was all but over.

As the final seconds ticked away, the Cougars began congratulating each other as only a team that had waited 20 years to do it could. BYU followers, half-expecting this win yet not believing it had really happened, began streaming out of the stands to celebrate with the team.

The Cougars had won the game both on the scoreboard and the field. They gained 152 yards on the ground (just five by passing) to Utah's 80. Total yardage was 157-117 in BYU's favor. The offense had been erratic, but came through in the clutch. The defense had been brilliant all game, particularly in its second-half stands deep in BYU territory. Overall, it was a gritty, totally inartistic performance by the team. But it was a win, something that had never been accomplished against Utah before.

And the man who had told his team for weeks that they'd be basking in this very moment could finally relax. Floyd Millet had suffered through an afternoon filled with pregame anxieties and a contest containing as many twists of plot and irony as the best mystery thriller.

Time had finally run out on Utah, and 20 years of pent-up BYU emotion exploded into a gala celebration on the field.

Millet strode toward the locker room, pleased with not just the win, but the way his players did it.

They ran right at, and over, Utah.

Ike Armstrong, quoted in Sunday's Salt Lake *Tribune,* was philosophical in defeat: "I guess the world won't come to an end because we lost. We've had our share of wins and if we can't take it, we shouldn't be playing the game." His postgame remark to the ex-Utah player, now BYU assistant coach, Paul Rose, was a little more to the point: "You certainly undercut us, didn't you?" Ike was smiling when he said it, and Rose hoped he was jesting.

Millet was equally philosophical about the win: "It had to happen sometime and I guess I was just lucky to come along at the right time. I'm proud of the boys; they wanted this and they went out to get it."

BYU fans were far from reflective about their victory. They immediately headed, en masse, for the goal posts and started to tear them down. Utah boosters, understandably in a bad mood, were just as anxious not to see their home turf defiled. Another game of sorts began. BYU people tried, through force and stratagem, to transport a permanent memento of their win back to Provo, while Ute backers were just as energetic in preventing it from happening.

What followed in the next hour was a wild melee that was both comic and tragic, but one that only occasionally crossed over the dangerous line leading to riot. It was all worthy of a movie.

BYU fans managed to get the south goal posts taken down, but were prevented from taking more than a handful of chips and splinters from it. (They wanted the whole thing.) As the opposing groups struggled, like rugby players massed together, police started moving in to break it up.

An alert University of Utah band began playing "The Star-Spangled Banner." It froze the police to attention, but did nothing to stop the action around the goal posts. Meanwhile, another BYU group sneaked around and began taking down the goal posts on the other side of the field. They had transported them, intact, halfway up the hill beside the stadium before being nabbed by Ute supporters.

The whole affair ended rather peacefully with the Utes winning this second game, and only the downed goal posts and some blackened eyes and bloodied noses remaining as evidence. Cougar fans did manage to get enough of the posts back to Provo to provide the coaches and many of the players with their own small pieces.

Millet still has his—complete with an inscription

of the date, score, place and list of the 45 players on his team.

Most of the players took the victory in stride — they were too tired to do otherwise. Sixty minutes of intense, hard-hitting football had turned them into weary, battered, but happy people. BYU fans provided most of the fuel for the celebration. While the battle of the goal posts raged on the field, most of the players removed their soiled uniforms, dressed in street clothes and patiently waited for the fracas to end.

The battle, clearly, had been won in the trenches. The line's game-long play won lavish praise from the coaches. Bird and Call had come back from painful injuries to turn in strong efforts at tackle. Call had a special pad prepared to help protect his hip from further injury. "I had to practically take my pants half off to adjust the thing all game," he recalls. It was still painful, but he played mightily, his blocked kick setting up BYU's winning touchdown. End Mike Mills also received frequent praise. But the game ball went to Nilsen, who snapped from center flawlessly all day and anchored a stingy defense at linebacker. Nilsen, after an eight-year coaching career (football assistant) at the Y, gave the ball back to the university. It has a permanent place in the football trophy case.

Eddie Kimball's guests had gathered and the San Diego victory party started. But it was well after midnight before an open long-distance line to Salt Lake City could be found. The Salt Lake *Tribune* answered the oft-attempted call. The score of the BYU-Utah football game? BYU 12, Utah 7.

"You'd have thought we were right there at the game," says the proud coach. "We were yelling and clapping . . . It was bedlam . . . It was a great moment for me."

A dozen people may not have matched the enthusiasm produced by thousands of fans and the entire city of Provo, but there weren't many happier people in the world that late Saturday night than Eddie Kimball.

On the front page of Sunday's Provo *Daily Herald*, just above the headlines "U.S. Destroys 48 German Planes in Mass Attack," and "Senate Enacts Biggest Tax Bill in U.S. History," was a huge line of type stretching across the top of the page, proclaiming what many Provo residents thought was October 10's biggest event: "Cougars Humble Utes, 12-7."

Monday was officially proclaimed a day of celebration by Provo Mayor Maurice Harding. You can imagine what *that* was like. "These guys own the town," said an admiring Rose of his team.

Telegrams began streaming in from servicemen all over the world as news spread of the historic win. Millet has kept them all.

Strangely enough, BYU and Utah headed in totally unexpected directions after the big game. Utah, whose 0-3 start was the worst since 1925, woke up to win its last six games, most of them convincingly. It won the conference championship.

BYU lost its final four games, most of them convincingly, including one to a powerhouse group called the Fort Douglas Military Police. (Are they the same ones who tried to break up the post-game melee?) It was obvious the team peaked for Utah, and as injuries claimed more and more players and the war claimed still others, it became harder with each passing week to field a competitive squad. The final game against Colorado State was mutually called off because of a lack of players.

BYU finished a dismal 2-5 for the year. It beat the conference champion (Utah) and lost to the only team to finish below it in the standings (Wyoming). But Millet's mission had been accomplished, and the 1942 team will be forever known as the first squad to beat Utah.

Football was discontinued during the years 1943-45 because of the war. (Utah continued its program.) Rose returned to Murray, and for the remainder of the war Millet was placed in charge of physical fitness programs for several hundred Army Air Corps soldiers who trained at BYU.

Eddie Kimball enthusiastically returned to coach the 1946 BYU football team. It was, literally, a veteran squad of considerable talent. Of the 69 players, 53 had served in World War II. He had so many players, in fact, he had to create a junior varsity squad, coached by Floyd Millet. But it was back to status quo against Utah. The Utes drubbed the Cougars 35-6 in the revival of the rivalry. Kimball coached the team two more years before becoming the athletic director full time. BYU lost to Utah 28-6 and 30-0 in those seasons.

Still, no one could steal the one moment of triumph he enjoyed after his team's biggest game of the year. Ironically, it came late on a Saturday night with a small group of friends in faraway San Diego.

5

The First Championship

"From the top of the Rockies I send my love and blessing. Many thousands share my pride in your record. I have faith in your abilities. Play clean, play hard, play fair, play to win. God bless you.

— President George Albert Smith"

Except for the muted sounds of the crowd above, it was quiet in the locker room at Madison Square Garden as BYU basketball coach Stan Watts finished reading the telegram from the LDS leader.

He had been reading from a handful of messages wishing them well, not realizing he had received one from the Church President until he read it. While undoubtedly some team members were too excited to pay much notice, others were visibly moved. Minutes before the championship game of the 1951 National Invitation Tournament the Cougars were on the brink of the first major national breakthrough in their sports history.

Following a semifinal win over Seton Hall two days before, a number of telegrams had arrived from prominent sources: the governor of Wyoming, the Laramie and Evanston chambers of commerce, the studentbody of Colorado A&M. But the one from President Smith had the most profound effect. "I could tell they were impressed," Watts would remember 33 years later. "They were quiet, but you could see they were impressed they would get a telegram from such a busy and important man. It really inspired them."

It was perhaps then they realized how far they had come. After all, BYU was only a small institution with under 6,000 students, obscurely tucked beneath the Wasatch Mountains of Utah. And though the Cougars had carried on successfully for some time in the Mountain States, this was their first bid to the prestigious NIT, their first chance at national exposure.

There would be other seasons and other players to bring BYU fame and make it a major sports institution, but that would come later.

The beginnings were there in New York, during that breathless March of 1951.

It is an interesting coincidence that BYU has won the NIT twice and both times the team made a summer basketball tour of South America prior to the regular season.

On the 1950 trip the Cougars were a novelty in the Southern Hemisphere; tall, blond boys playing a game that people knew very little about in countries where soccer was usually the major draw. But the communities found the Americans intriguing and the game fascinating.

In one South American town a small crowd had gathered around the Cougar players when someone handed a ball to Mel Hutchins, the team's center, asking him to make a shot. Despite his street shoes, slacks and jacket, he slam-dunked the ball, bringing a gasp of gleeful surprise from the onlookers, who had never seen such a feat. Before long they were called the "Kings of Basketball" in the towns they visited.

Slam-dunking the ball on one South American court, though, ranged from monumental feat to child's play. During the game the Cougars discovered the hoop they were shooting at was six inches or more higher than the regulation 10 feet. After changing ends at halftime they came out to find the other basket raised and their opponents' lowered.

At times the crowds became overwrought in close games against the big Americans, and the Cougars were cautioned to go for "blowouts" so the locals wouldn't get too involved in the outcome.

BYU won all 12 games handily.

While the competition wasn't much, the experience of playing in strange gyms before hostile crowds and spending every waking hour together produced a tight-knit team and the most successful season in the history of BYU's basketball program.

While playing conditions were better at home, they were a long way from ideal. BYU had no home gym. The million-dollar Smith Fieldhouse wouldn't be ready for a year, and the team had to practice in an old gym on the third floor of a campus building, a facility with the backboards nailed right against the walls. Watts would drive recruits around campus and past the gym as quickly as he could, saying, "That's where we practice."

The closest thing to home territory was the tiny Springville High gym with a 1,700 seating capacity. BYU played four games there that year, fans crowding in so tight their feet stuck out over the boundary lines. Other teams in the conference complained about the court, which was much smaller than a college gym, to the point that BYU arranged to use the University of Utah Nielsen Fieldhouse the remainder of the season. Thus, BYU played 10 "home" games in the home of the Redskins, the most taxing the four they played against Utah.

And sometimes the crowds could get over-wrought there, too.

Utah and BYU each won two turbulent games against each other that year. At times it was hard to tell which side the crowd favored, as many BYU fans crowded into the Utah fieldhouse to watch the two old rivals.

During one of the games things escalated quickly and emotions both on the court and in the stands ran high. Roland Minson, the team's leading scorer, always drew his share of heckling from the crowd, though it rarely affected him. But that night he was called on a crucial foul late in the game which he considered highly questionable. In an uncharacter-istic move, he walked deliberately to the official, put his arm around him and said, "Go ahead. Give him three pitches. Give him four!"

Having gotten that off his chest, Minson wheeled squarely into the path of a Utah cheerleader — who he later learned was on the wrestling team as well.

"He was right in my face," remembers Minson. "In fact, he had his hand dropped back like he was going to hit me and I remember being very surprised that he was so upset. I was cooled off . . ."

People pressed down onto the court as officials struggled to keep order. Suddenly over Minson's right shoulder shot a brown-suited arm, clipping the burly cheerleader squarely on the chin, knocking him out with one punch. Turning around, Minson was greeted by the sight of a longtime Provo businessman and BYU booster, rather slight of build, drawing back from his knockout punch.

Minson's mother, a devoted follower of the Cougars, went outside for a brick to put in her purse, should the need arise. She was unable to find one and by the time she returned to the gym the court was roped off and order restored. As she approached the playing floor a police officer she didn't know stopped her. "Now, Sister Minson," he said softly, "don't you worry. Your son just knocked that cheerleader out."

Basketball was a much different game in 1951. BYU was called a fast-paced running team, yet averaged only 65 points a game. Some of the players had developed jump shots while others relied heavily on hooks and two-handed set shots. Zone defenses were practically nonexistent.

What was considered fine shooting then would be an embarrassment today. As a team that year BYU shot only 35 percent, its opponents under 30 percent.

The Cougars won the Skyline Conference title for the second time in as many years since Watts had become head coach. The conference crown earned them an NCAA berth.

BYU was an unusually unselfish team, even for a day when many team players were available and not so many hotshots. Their experience in South America and a season of games in foreign gyms not only gave them an overall 28-9 record that year, but prepared them well for playing in New York. They climbed as high as a No. 3 national ranking in some polls.

Most visible of the Cougars was 6-foot-5 center Mel Hutchins—Hutch the Clutch—averaging 15.4 points and 12.7 rebounds a game. Hutchins was named a *Look* magazine all-America and called by the magazine "probably the most stylish player in the country."

If the public wasn't convinced as a whole, at least most of the BYU coeds were. Watts recounts how the girls would attend the games "just to see Mel," such were his good looks.

Despite his obvious offensive skills—an extremely good corner set-shot as well as the usual array of inside shots—Hutchins was most valuable for his defense. His economy of moves was so well orchestrated that early in his career some observers accused him of loafing. "He had such fluidity," says Watts. "He made things look so easy."

Although a good leaper, Hutchins also had great speed and timing and regularly blocked shots by players taller than he. Early in his career he was scolded by BYU coach Floyd Millet for not playing defense as well as he should, so, after the timeout, he picked out a hook shot by the man he was guarding and swatted it into the second tier of the stands.

Hutchins' abilities were not all natural, however. His defensive skills, which carried him through his professional career, were learned guarding a 5-foot-10 friend through high school and college, and who taught Hutchins how to stay with smaller men. When Hutchins was put in against a bigger man, his quickness and timing usually prevailed.

The other star BYU player was Minson—The Cat. He was a crowd-pleaser who played with eye-catching offensive flair. Often Hutchins went to the wing for his patented outside shot, drawing the opposing big man with him. Then Minson would slide into the post, usually scoring with ease against his

Mel Hutchins (left) and Roland Minson proved to be most valuable in BYU's history-making 1950-51 hoop season.

While Roland Minson (with ball) provided style, teammate Boyd Jarman (15) added perspective when they got to N.Y.

own man. At 6 feet Minson was a fine jump shooter but also moved well near the basket.

Though Minson was the team's top scorer, Hutchins was better known as they entered the NIT. It was Hutchins who had previously been selected to play in the prestigious East-West all-star game; Minson wasn't invited until he had taken the East by storm during the NIT.

The other starters were steady 6-foot-1 forward Joe Richey, a sophomore; junior guard Jerry Romney, 6-3; and sophomore guard Harold Christensen, 6-1. Though Christensen was just a sophomore, he had good leadership ability and exerted a steadying influence on the team, rarely making a bad pass or taking a poor shot.

Despite the star status afforded Hutchins and Minson, they were never ball-hogging bores, but rather team-oriented players. The weeks in South America had molded the team into a fast and firm group of friends.

All were fond of Watts, even the ones who warmed the bench. The young coach, in his second year leading the Cougars, had won the Skyline Conference title both seasons. He could get upset occasionally, but did not berate his players and they respected his judgment.

Watts could laugh with his players, which put them at ease. On a train to Laramie to play the University of Wyoming one night the team was involved in a pillow fight in a club car and, hearing the noise, Watts came down to see what was going on. Just as he opened the door Hutchins threw a pillow that caught the coach squarely in the face. Watts merely grinned, "You'd better get a little better aim, Hutch."

Watts's easy style was reflected in the team. Most were outgoing and confident, polite and extremely conscious of their LDS image. And they were obedient. "You tell them to go get a crew cut and the next day they'd be back with a crew cut," says Watts.

BYU began the season by winning its first four games before taking on one of the most feared opponents in the country: City College of New York. CCNY had won both the NIT and NCAA tourneys the year before and, to make things even more difficult, the game would be played in Madison Square Garden.

The Cougars went to New York that December, reveling in the image of country boys in the big city. Reserve center Boyd Jarman, not long off the ranch in Wyoming, stepped into the empty Madison Square Garden for practice the first day in New York. He slowly looked up into the dimly lit top rows of the arena and drawled, "Boy, this barn sure will hold a lot of hay."

There was no televising of college games then and few films available. Schools hired scouting services to get information and Watts had had his own team scouted for weaknesses. Just how good CCNY was, or BYU for that matter, was uncertain.

But BYU gave CCNY, and the Garden crowd, enough to think about. The Cougars lost by just two points. And it was in that game they began to realize how good they were and to sense there was more, much more, to come.

College basketball badly needed heroes that year. During the days preceding the NIT a scandal had tarnished the sport, more than a dozen New York area players having become involved in fixing games.

What New York needed right then was a clean basketball team, a team with players that didn't swear, didn't smoke, didn't drink and didn't fix games. No wonder the NIT invited BYU.

At that time the NIT enjoyed great status. Held the week before the NCAAs, it brought together the elite college teams—no automatic berths, just invitations.

BYU had made a lasting impression on the basketball community early that season when the Cougars had nearly beaten CCNY. That, combined with their conference championship, their 24-7 record, and their high-profile stars Hutchins and Minson, officials knew would draw well.

Brigham Young was the No. 3 seeded team in the tournament, behind St. John's and North Carolina State and ahead of the only other seeded team, Arizona.

Though BYU's first opponent, St. Louis University, was unseeded, it was considered the most dangerous of all the unseeded teams, having beaten LaSalle 73-61 to advance to the quarterfinals. The Billikens were led by Ray Sonnenberg, who scored 18 points against LaSalle.

But Monday's opener for the Cougars was not even close, BYU moving to a 75-58 win on Minson's showy 28-point performance. The Provo team had entered the contest a two-point favorite but its running game was working well from the start and the defense even better.

The lead widened to 17 points, 52-35, before St. Louis made a charge that cut the lead to eight. But that was as close as the Billikens got.

Minson scored 15 of his points in the first half, boosting BYU to a comfortable 38-21 lead. Sonnenberg, who had a fine offensive day with 20 points, didn't fare so well defensively, as he was assigned to Minson. Though nearly five inches taller than Minson, he was unable to stop the scoring. During the game three players tried their hand at halting Minson, all unsuccessfully. Finally (according to *Deseret News* writer Hack Miller) during a timeout Billiken coach Ed Hickey told his players: "We've tried three men on Minson and can't stop him. Now I'm asking for volunteers. Anyone else want to try him?"

Nobody volunteered.

"We were really surprised," Hickey told reporters afterward. "Mel Hutchins is a terrific player — both as a shooter and rebounder — but Rollie Minson caught us napping. I thought we did a fair job guarding Hutchins but we couldn't handle Minson."

Nor could anyone else.

After getting past St. Louis BYU's stock rose. The Cougars were already mentioned by some as a favorite to win the tourney, a finalist by most. But the next opponent wouldn't be as easily dealt with as St. Louis.

While Stan Watts had predicted before the St. Louis game his team would make the finals if they got past the Billikens, the Cougars' opponent in Game 2, Seton Hall, was not buying it.

What the Pirates lacked in ranking, they made up in intimidation. They had upset No. 2 seed North Carolina State Tuesday and their center was the biggest man in the tournament, 6-10 Wally Dukes, a sophomore who had scored 19 points and taken in 25 rebounds in the previous game.

Prior to the game Pirates' coach Honey Russell told United Press, "If we continue to play as well as we have I think we can do it against Brigham Young — although it will be tougher [than the previous tournament wins over Beloit and North Carolina State]."

The young Dukes was still learning what he could do against people smaller than he. He was all legs and elbows, but he figured he could run most any opponent to death. "We may have to put stilts on Hutchins so he can handle Dukes," Watts said.

Of perhaps more concern than Dukes, though, was the condition of a couple of BYU players. Hutchins had a sore wrist, at first thought to be fractured, but by game time he was well. And Richey had been hit with the flu; but he, too, seemed recovered by Thursday night.

Despite having a game behind them the Cougars appeared tight at the start as Seton Hall jumped ahead 8-2 in the first six minutes. But BYU opened up the fast break to close the lead while Hutchins began working on Dukes inside. BYU tied the score at 10 and Hutchins and Minson moved the Cougars ahead 16-10. BYU kept a 33-26 halftime lead and stayed with it comfortably to win 69-59.

While Hutchins played well defensively, allowing Dukes only six of his 18 shots, the BYU center didn't get away unaffected. He fouled out in the second half, but Dick Jones was exceptional in relief, holding Dukes to a single field goal the last several minutes.

Seton Hall mustered a rally to within nine points with nine minutes left, but it was a last gasp.

Minson was again the main event with 26 points, while Romney and Richey got 14 and 16 points, respectively. Hutchins' defensive assignment had taken its toll as he finished with only eight points.

It had taken the Cougars well into the second game to overcome some of the nerves of playing in a national tournament. Now they could worry about the nerves that come with playing for a national championship.

BYU's win over Seton Hall and Dayton's victory over St. John's thoroughly wrecked the promoters' dreams of an all-New York-area championship series.

Though Dayton didn't have anyone as big as Dukes to contend with, the Flyers were on a major roll, coming from nowhere to make the title game. Their hopes were riding on the play of 6-foot-7 Don Meineke, said by many to be the best player in the tournament.

Though Meineke scored just 11 points against St. John's, he had buried 37 points in the upset win over Arizona. The Flyers had beaten the No. 1 and No. 4 teams in the tournament; thus, the prospect of beating BYU didn't seem remote to them in the least.

In fact, Meineke, who in the pros actually became Hutchins's roommate, used to kid him: "Aw, you stymied us. You took away our offense: Me."

Despite being a four- to five-point underdog, Dayton felt it was a shoo-in for the title. The Flyers had talked to team members from CCNY and been told they would have no trouble handling BYU.

Dayton was aggressive and Meineke was a one-man attack. Aside from him there was only one player BYU had cause to be concerned over and that was 6-1, 226-pound Leland Norris, a blocky guard with a dangerous outside shot.

Indeed, it was Norris who would hurt the Cougars most.

It was, at last, Saturday and the Cougars met for their pregame meal, the talk getting around to who the Most Valuable Player of the tournament would be. Perhaps Minson, who had played so flawlessly. Or Hutchins, who had led BYU in rebounding and handled the best player from each team defensively.

Or Meineke, the Flyers' big gun, who could pour in points faster than anyone in the tournament.

Hutchins looked slightly amused by the talk until someone asked him what he thought. Then he just grinned. "I'll tell you one thing," he said. "It isn't going to be Meineke."

They had waited through an overtime and two trips down the corridor from the locker room for the championship of the 1951 National Invitation Tournament to begin, their nerves pulling at them, turning their palms cold.

Finally the overtime consolation game ended and the teams took the court for warmups. The arena dimmed for player introductions under the spotlight. Only the sighing of the crowd in the darkness and the flickering cigarette embers that disappeared into the distance reminded them they were actually there, in The Garden, and this would be their night of destiny — or disappointment.

One by one the players' names were called as they dribbled a ball out to mid-court under the embarrassing glare of the spotlight: Romney, Christensen, Richey, Minson, Hutchins. "I remember being so nervous I didn't know if I was going to kick the ball clear up into the stands or not," Christensen would recall.

Nobody kicked the ball. That, they considered a good sign.

Maybe a great one.

Danny Ainge's charge into the nation's consciousness in 1981 during the NCAA tournament wasn't wholly an original act. Each year someone becomes the focus of the public and press. Ainge's performance, for that matter, wasn't the first time a

BYU player had riveted the nation's attention on himself; Roland Minson had preceded Ainge by 30 years.

Though Minson played without the benefit of national television coverage, by the time he ended the tournament virtually every college basketball fan in the country knew his name.

The New York *Times* called him the "Blond Bombshell" as his flashy style captured the attention of the huge New York press contingent.

He was never better than that final night as BYU cruised to a 62-43 victory.

The *Times* described his performance as "by far the greatest individual showing of the campaign." It continued: "Forget, if you can, the 26 points the co-captain sent through the nets. Minimize his 15 rebounds, his numerous interceptions and assists. Ignore his eye-catching dribbling and his ability to feint the defense out of position. But if you do, you will be alone."

Many said Minson's three-game performance was the greatest in the 14-year history of the tournament.

Dayton went ahead 4-0 in the game's first minute, the Flyers fast breaking and BYU playing, curiously, slower than in either previous game. Dayton extended its lead to 24-18, which the Flyers fully expected to expand.

Minson, though, remained cool, scoring 12 first-half points in a dazzling array of shots: hooks, jumpers, drives, set shots, clearly unnerving Dayton.

Meanwhile, Hutchins had the thankless job of guarding Meineke and, as he had predicted, making sure that Meineke didn't win the MVP. Though a good shot, the Ohio star used a short half hook which Hutchins blocked with startling ease several times. Too, Meineke was slow and Hutchins spent the entire game slapping the ball away before Meineke could even get his shot off.

The end result: Meineke took just ten shots and hit only one, while Hutchins himself scored six in the highly publicized matchup.

So close was Hutchins in guarding Meineke that during the second half the Dayton star leaned near him and said, "I'm going out for a drink. Don't follow me to the fountain. You just stay away."

BYU remained poised despite the early deficit and scored four points in a row to take a 28-26 half-time lead. Dayton had led much of the way, but Norris, not Meineke, had done the damage. With 20 points for the game, he was the only Flyer to threaten the Cougars.

The second half was barely a contest. Hutchins continued to throttle Meineke while Minson turned heads with his shooting and passing. But until six minutes were left in the game Dayton still remained close enough to win. BYU scored 11 straight points, seven by Minson, and the Cougars had a safe 50-31 lead to ride home on.

BYU's first national title of any kind touched off the predictable delirium in Provo. The results were flashed across a movie screen and people began spilling out the doors into the streets and joining others in a snake dance. Students drove cars through the business district, honking horns and screaming.

The *Deseret News* even carried a story of a wedding in Payson, the celebration delayed while the entire party listened to the game. After the final buzzer the festivities continued.

While there was much to celebrate, the Cougars sadly had little time to enjoy it. They were due the next week in Kansas City to continue their quest to sweep the college basketball tournaments by winning the NCAAs. They had dinner in a fine restaurant, called home and went to bed. On Sunday they rested and on Monday were thinking of the upcoming tournament.

The Cougars beat San Jose State in their first game of the NCAAs, but a nearly team-wide bout with the flu and an ankle injury to the irreplaceable Hutchins played a part in their losses to Kansas State and Washington that ended the season.

Minson, the NIT Most Valuable Player, joined Hutchins a week later in New York for the East-West all-star game. Hutchins had told Minson after the NIT awards had been handed out, "This one's yours and you deserve it, but the next one (at the all-star game) is mine."

And it was. BYU got one last fleeting moment of publicity when Hutchins was named MVP of the all-star game.

Despite the disappointment of coming home after a loss—BYU had flown directly to Kansas City after winning the NIT—it didn't dampen enthusiasm in Provo. A throng of well-wishers and a band greeted the team as the train arrived Monday at 7:15 A.M. after the NCAA tourney play was over.

Days followed filled with talks, banquets and awards, so many that there was only fleeting sadness at not getting the NCAA title, too. They lost the double sweep, but they did bring to BYU its first nationally recognized title. And the first is always the sweetest.

6

Friday Night Fever in Houston

99 . . . 100 . . . 101 . . . 102 . . .

As Marc Wilson's temperature rose, his hopes sank. With every degree of his fever seemingly went a piece of his promising career.

The illness that enveloped the BYU quarterback played a cruel game not unlike a roulette with flower petals: "He will play . . . he won't play . . . he will play . . . he won't play . . ." The petals were rapidly disappearing, and so were his chances of playing.

As Wilson lay helpless in a hotel bed, hot and miserable as the Texas night outside, his BYU teammates were at Houston's Rice Stadium, ambitiously preparing for the following night's football game.

But this wouldn't be just any football game. It was Friday, September 7, 1979, and the Cougars were tuning up for Texas A&M, a national power judged as the season started to be anywhere from the 9th to 14th best college football team in the country. It was, simply, The Most Important Football Game In BYU History—a long-awaited chance for the Cougars to prove they could play with (and maybe even beat) national-caliber competition.

With less than 24 hours to game time, it didn't take a 102-degree fever to chill Wilson as he considered his predicament.

BYU was fortunate to have a *surviving* returning quarterback, let alone one with Wilson's predicted all-America credentials.

Still basking in the preseason assessments of his abilities and prospects, Wilson left for a camping trip to Idaho's rugged Sawtooth Mountains. It was to be one last fling before demanding fall workouts began. While in this remote wilderness his appendix burst. He was rushed to a hospital barely in time to save his life. Surgery on BYU's starting quarterback was performed August 21, only two and a half weeks before his senior-year debut against Texas A&M.

Wilson had as much to prove in this game as anyone. After a sensational sophomore year (in his first game against Colorado State, he passed for seven touchdowns and ran for an eighth), Wilson struggled through the 1978 season, sharing quarterbacking duties with promising and super-confident sophomore Jim McMahon.

This season would be Wilson's last, and he wanted to go out big. He was determined to prove in the Texas A&M game that he could lead BYU's football team full time, that the Cougars *were* a legitimate national power and that he, personally, was worthy of consideration for a professional football career.

With all this on the line, Wilson wasn't about to let even a near-fatal burst appendix stand in his way. His recovery was quick and remarkable. Still, the player wearing No. 6 who showed up to practice barely one week before his "big-chance" game in Houston was the mere skeletal remains of Marc Wilson. He weighed more than 20 pounds less than his normal playing weight of 205, a load ill-suited to his 6-foot-5 frame. He was weak and worn down by illness. But he was also determined to quarterback the biggest game of his life the following Saturday night.

In practice that week he earned the chance. He would fly to Houston with the team and give it a try. If it didn't work out, there was always Jim McMahon waiting on the sidelines . . .

And now this—the mysterious malady that struck him late in the week, leaving him gripped with pain and burning with fever. It may have been the flu or a delayed infection from his appendectomy. Whatever it was, it represented another major obstacle to his already-remarkable climb back to the helm of the Cougar offense. Would this, now, keep him from playing tomorrow night?

As Wilson continued his lonely struggle in the Astrodome Marriott, the team's feverish preparations also continued two miles to the north at Rice Stadium.

Wilson knew exactly what was happening. The Cougars were drawing up "Plan B" in the increasingly likely chance he couldn't play. And performing the role of quarterback at this spirited workout was Jim McMahon. Though McMahon had been asked to sit out Wilson's senior year, he was ready, gimpy knee and all, to take charge of the team if called on.

Who would lead the Cougar offense tomorrow night? The team didn't know. But if this uncertainty affected morale, it wasn't apparent. "We've come too far for it to matter who plays quarterback," said reserve wide receiver Kent Tingey. "The show will still have to go on tomorrow night."

The BYU team *had* come a long way—1,400 miles—to play this game. But Tingey was speaking figuratively—this was a chance to prove the BYU program had come of age.

The entire team had been eagerly awaiting this game for months. It was foremost on the players' minds from the start of spring practice and often dominated conversations between team members. Tight end Clay Brown even had a T-shirt made in late spring that brashly promised a BYU victory.

The rare chance to play a nationally recognized powerhouse sent spirits soaring and drove the team to what Coach LaVell Edwards called perhaps the best practice camp he'd ever seen. "It was obvious they had this goal (beating A&M) in mind from the beginning," he said.

To understand the players' enthusiasm, you'd need to know the status of BYU football in 1979. The Cougars were roaring for national respect on the heels of three straight nine-win seasons. But what they got in return was general skepticism. "Anyone can win nine games a year in the Western Athletic Conference." "Yeah, but who have you played?" "BYU would be an also-ran in most better conferences." The respect and recognition the emerging BYU program craved just wasn't there.

So the Cougars of 1979 had something to prove. They felt they could play with anyone in the nation and even win their share of games against the top teams.

And why not? While BYU's teams were accorded little national respect, Marc Wilson was still being hailed as one of the nation's best returning college quarterbacks. And possessing a talented corps of receivers to throw to, and an intricate, high-powered offense that tied defenses in knots all around the western United States, BYU felt it was a force to be reckoned with.

Texas A&M would be a formidable foe to test that force. In tailback Curtis Dickey, fullback George Woodard and quarterback Mike Mosley, A&M boasted one of the best running attacks in the country. And a solid defense anchored by Jacob Green (a preseason candidate for the Outland award, the linemen's version of the coveted Heisman) would not be easy for the Cougars to score against.

So as BYU prepared for A&M, it knew exactly what was at stake. A good performance would earn the football program the respect it wanted; a poor performance might set that back years.

No one was more aware of this do-or-die situation than the surprise visitor to the Astrodome Marriott Friday — Gifford Nielsen. The former BYU great was now a popular second-year quarterback for the National Football League's Houston Oilers.

"Don't let me down," Nielsen told the coaches and players he was able to see. "Go and play your hearts out. I'm behind you."

Nielsen was extremely interested in the game's outcome. He and his BYU colleagues of a few years ago had helped build the football foundation that they hoped would now be unveiled as a "complete building" against Texas A&M.

Also, he was the lone alum from BYU, and one of very few WAC players, on a team loaded with talent from the nation's top football conferences, including

Texas A&M's Southwest Conference. "A&M will drill them." "BYU plays a 'patsy' schedule." "They'll never win down here." This had been Nielsen's steady diet from Oiler teammates for the entire week.

But Nielsen was confident, so much so that he wagered a dinner at a popular Houston seafood restaurant on the outcome. The person most responsible for earning Nielsen his dinner, Marc Wilson, was too ill to see his old teammate and friend. So Nielsen left for home, bound later for an important game of his own in Pittsburgh. But he didn't leave without setting the Cougars up with an item that proved to be more important than he realized—one that would help the BYU quarterback dodge tough A&M defensive bullets all night—a protective "flak jacket."

If there was confusion in the BYU camp over who would quarterback the team Saturday night, the answer was perfectly clear to Marc Wilson: "Maybe others were wondering, but I knew I was going to play. It was my senior year; it was my last chance."

All during his troubling Friday night he had "willed" himself to play. And as it had after his ruptured appendix, will conquered illness and he pronounced himself fit to play Saturday morning. The fever was gone.

But it was a weak, 25-pound-underweight quarterback who asked to be thrown into the battle. The decision wasn't easy. BYU wanted to "red-shirt" McMahon, who was recovering from knee surgery himself. This would ensure the Cougars a quality quarterback for two years after Wilson's departure. If McMahon were forced to play, he would have just one more year after this one, and the team would again be faced with the co-starter nightmare of 1978.

On the other hand, a weakened Wilson, even with a flak jacket, would be more vulnerable to injury, especially at the hands of a physical team such as Texas A&M. The coaches didn't want to see a career end, either.

Then there was the game. Sure, it was *just* an intersectional, non-conference game, and everyone was downplaying its importance. But the game really *was* important to BYU, and it needed a fit quarterback to lead the team.

All along, Wilson kept insisting he could play, so the decision was finally made: Marc, wearing a flak jacket Gifford Nielsen had arranged for him to get, would start the game.

Uncertainty surrounding Wilson's physical condition, and an excellent A&M team, were just two obstacles separating the Cougars from their desired "good showing." Much had been made about two other factors observers predicted would hamper the visitors from Provo.

The first was Mother Nature. Houston had rolled out its best heat and humidity to frustrate another invading football team. The game-time temperature of 85 was coupled with 70 percent humidity. The press predicted the Cougars (and especially their recovering quarterback) would eventually be worn down by the sultry conditions. It would feel like a sauna to players accustomed to the dry, cool evening air of the Rocky Mountains. Ironically, just down the street from BYU's hotel, the Houston Astros were playing baseball in the climate-controlled comfort of the Astrodome. But the Cougars would have to sweat it out.

A second handicap would be Texas A&M's "12th man"—the crowd. The game was being played at "neutral" Rice Stadium because A&M's 20,000-seat stadium expansion wasn't quite ready. But the few hundred BYU supporters at the game would still be swallowed up by more than 40,000 Aggie boosters making the 100-mile drive from College Station southeast to Houston. A&M fans are among the nation's most vocal and are known for their tradition of standing during entire games. Surely the Cougars would be intimidated by such a rabid throng.

Rice Stadium was already awash with excitement as Mike Lacey and Tim Halverson pulled white and blue jerseys over their shoulder pads. But not all of the emotion emanated from the rapidly assembling crowd. The BYU dressing room was filled with a near-white heat of anticipation. The months and months of waiting were almost over; the game would soon begin.

As Lacey and Halverson looked around them they saw potential all-conference and even all-America candidates getting ready for the game— categories neither of these two players fit into.

Lacey was a highly recruited linebacker, a high school all-America, from Rancho Cordova, California. Several Pacific Coast football powers sought his talents, but his LDS roots brought him to BYU. He played sparingly as a freshman, then went on a mission to Costa Rica and returned to a team overloaded with linebacking talent. He decided to sit out a year, then try his hand at fullback, a position where the Cougars needed help.

Halverson was somewhat less heralded as he completed his high school career in West Covina, California. Still, he had earned a starting spot in BYU's defensive backfield as a sophomore. Then,

Though twenty pounds underweight against Texas A&M, Marc Wilson contributed heavily to Coach LaVell Edwards's game plan.

like Lacey, he departed for a mission — to Nagoya, Japan — and came back to find all the starting positions filled.

In pregame interviews discussing BYU players who might help lead their team to victory that night, Mike Lacey's and Tim Halverson's names weren't mentioned. In fact, as the underdog Cougars sprinted onto the field, it looked like special-teams duty would be the primary assignment for these two players. Surely there was no hero material here.

Underdogs the Cougars certainly were. When Brent Johnson approached the ball for the game's opening kickoff, his team was *favored* to lose by

12-16 points. Many BYU followers watching the game on television in Utah would have considered a seven-point loss a moral victory.

The first quarter did nothing to raise their hopes. Marc Wilson dropped back to unleash the deadly passing attack nine times. Five of those passes fell incomplete, two were never thrown because of sacks and one was intercepted. The one pass that was caught netted just two yards.

BYU earned first-down yardage only twice in that first quarter. One came via a 15-yard A&M penalty and the other on a nifty 20-yard scamper around right end by Homer Jones — but then he fumbled the ball away at the end of the play.

BYU's offense wasn't ineffective; it was non-existent.

*Tim Halverson (left) and Mike Lacey unexpectedly emerged as
key players in the final minutes of the game.*

Disaster was averted, thanks to punter Clay Brown and the defense. Brown, also the starting tight end, boomed punts of 64 and 49 yards to pin A&M deep in its own territory, once on the 1-yard line. Brown, in his punting role, was easily BYU's top offensive weapon in the first quarter.

And while yards came fairly easily for A&M, the Cougar defense was able to clamp down when needed. The Aggies' one touchdown drive, capped by a one-yard David Brothers dive midway through the quarter, required nine plays to cover just 35 yards. No other sustained drives were allowed, and explosive running back Curtis Dickey was held to bursts of short-to-moderate yardage.

But every silver lining must have a dark cloud, and BYU's defense suffered a serious blow late in that first quarter. As Dickey was slashing through the right side of the defense, linebacker Danny Frazier came over to make the stop after a six-yard gain. Frazier drove right into Dickey with a solid hit that forced the ball loose. BYU recovered the fumble. But it had also lost one of its potentially best line-backers ever. Frazier, who lay writhing in pain on the turf, had broken a vertebra in his neck. His football season, and career with BYU, had ended after just beginning. He managed to walk off the field, and it wasn't until X-rays were taken at the hospital that his plight was discovered. (Happily, the popular Frazier, BYU's only black LDS player at that time, recovered well and left for a mission four months later to Oakland, California. He later played basketball for BYU-Hawaii.)

Entering the second quarter, BYU was missing a starting linebacker, an offense and points. It was 7-0 A&M.

But the Cougars did have great field position—the Aggie 43-yard line—thanks to Brown's punting. Wilson went right to work. A 19-yard pass to Dan Plater highlighted a quick surge to inside the 10-yard line. Had it not been for a third-down delay of game penalty, the Cougars probably would have scored the tying touchdown. Instead, they had to settle for a short Brent Johnson field goal to cut the deficit to 7-3.

That short burst of efficiency would be all the BYU offense could manage for the rest of the half. Enter, again, the BYU defense.

A&M, starting from its own 31, swept down the field in five plays to the Cougar 7-yard line. A 14-3 Aggie lead seemed a sure bet. But BYU's defense started yielding yardage in bunches of two, rather than 10. A&M ended up with a fourth down and goal from the 1-yard line with about two minutes left in the half. There would be no field goal attempt. BYU's defense was momentarily staggered and would be easy prey for a touchdown, thought A&M coaches.

The Aggies' 12th man sent up a deafening roar, hoping its enthusiasm could help push a maroon-clad running back into the end zone. Mosley asked for quiet. He took the snap and turned to give it to freshman tailback Johnny Hector. Defensive back John Neal arrived at the same time. His hit popped the ball into the air just over the goal line. BYU still had to recover it to prevent a touchdown. Fellow defensive back Dave Francis was right there and gratefully covered the ball. The defensive had just prevented a sure touchdown, thanks to Neal and Francis.

But the heroics weren't over yet. Wilson's second interception with 41 seconds left handed A&M

another chance to score. On the last play of the half, Dickey, hoping to run out the clock, headed off left tackle. A quick cut to the right later, and he was in the open. Dickey was a fast man on a fast team — he was off to the races. But still another defensive back, Bill Schoepflin, pursued Dickey flawlessly and applied a sure tackle to the rampaging running back on the 25-yard line.

Was that a mirage Texas A&M players saw on the scoreboard as they jogged off the field at half-time? They had totally outplayed the sluggish Cougars, but the lights were arranged in a 7-3, not 21-3, pattern.

Neither the crowd nor the team were worried. A&M would start cashing in on its opportunities sooner or later, and the rout would be on.

No, the Cougars weren't pleased with their erratic first-half performance, but they were absolutely ecstatic about trailing by only four points.

"Hey, we can really play with these guys," exulted wide receiver Kent Tingey. "Just wait until our offense gets rolling!"

What did LaVell Edwards have to say at half-time? He said, "Let's just keep sticking to and executing the basics," recalled Mike Lacey, who was still anxious to get in and make his mark on the game. "Let's just keep sawing the wood."

Wilson was battered, but he and his flak jacket had survived the swarming A&M defense with no pieces missing. He was also encouraged. The physical abuse he had taken in the first half couldn't get any worse.

He was also confident he'd find the stamina to bring the Cougars back. "It was a weird feeling," he recalled later. "Sometimes when we fell behind I got a little anxious and wanted to get it all back right away. But I had the feeling all along we'd come back and win the game."

Wilson's confidence was sorely tested, and A&M's confidence vindicated in the initial minutes of the second half.

BYU received the opening kickoff, but was forced to punt after defensive end Jacob Green rushed Wilson into a third-down incompletion. Wilson was now a very uncharacteristic 6-for-14 in passing for just 40 yards.

Clay Brown's soaring 50-yard punt was negated by a 25 yard return by David Scott, and A&M took over near midfield. Seven running plays and one pass later, quarterback Mike Mosley swept into the end zone and A&M led 14-3. The scales of sports justice, tipped so long in BYU's favor, had swung back with a vengeance. A&M's 12th man was now clamoring for a Cougar pelt.

It wouldn't have taken much effort. The Cougars were skinning themselves. A 20-yard Marc Wilson-to-Dan Plater connection was all but wiped out with a 15-yard holding penalty on the next play. The drive came to a skidding halt.

Even another booming Brown punt that backed A&M to its own 15-yard line didn't keep a sense of impending doom from spreading among Cougar fans. A&M had seemingly solved BYU's defense. And BYU couldn't budge A&M's.

It was then that A&M coach Tom Wilson made two strategic decisions that ended up letting BYU off the hook. He inserted untested 18-year-old freshman quarterback Gary Kubiak, and several other reserves, into the game. And he started calling more passing plays, though his rushing offense was working well.

This combination first gave BYU good field position and, after the Cougars failed to move the ball again, then yielded something even more crucial. While rolling out to pass, Kubiak forgot something very important—the ball. Linebacker Glen Redd pounced on the neglected item, turning Kubiak's error into a turnover—a crushing one.

Someday, someone will figure out how a team that has struggled offensively for most of a game can suddenly catch fire and flow with efficiency. Until then, the reason for BYU's isolated 57-yard, one-minute explosion will remain a mystery.

Wilson first found running back Scott Phillips for eight yards, then connected with the same target for 12 yards. Boom—first down! The quarterback then spotted and hit wide receiver Bill Davis for 17 yards. Boom—first down! Plater was Wilson's next pass recipient, this one for 20 yards. Boom—touchdown! It was vintage BYU offense in a crucial situation, and it placed the Cougars right back in the game, 14-10, with less than two minutes to play in the third quarter. Wilson was in the midst of completing six consecutive passes.

Needless to say, veteran Aggie quarterback Mosley returned to the game posthaste. But he found an offense that had lost precious momentum in its previous two possessions, and it sputtered to a stop without a first down.

Wilson's twin 14-yard strikes to Brown and Davis sent BYU roaring back into Aggie territory. As the third quarter ended, the mood at Rice Stadium was quite different than at halftime. A worried buzz arose as BYU's aerial circus took off and its pilot,

Wilson, began shooting pinpoint passes to running backs, tight ends and split ends. A&M retained a 14-10 lead, but BYU had all-important momentum entering the deciding 15 minutes.

Only the most astute A&M fans in the stadium noted another factor working against the home team. Houston's oppressive humidity was taking its toll on the Aggies, not the Cougars. The more tired of the two teams entering the fourth quarter was clearly Texas A&M.

And as Wilson completed a six-yard pass to Phillips for a first down at the A&M 33-yard line, the buzz escalated to a low roar. But a passing team's worst enemy, a holding penalty, cost the Cougars that first down and a total of 25 yards. The drive couldn't recover from the shock.

After the teams traded possessions with only minor spurts of offense, A&M, tired or not, mounted its last charge. The first assault was carried out by speedy flanker David Scott, who returned a Brown punt 35 yards to the BYU 45-yard line. Dickey's salvo was next and he exploded with runs of 10 and 14 yards. A&M managed to penetrate to the BYU 16. But two fine defensive plays, one by Gary Kama and another by a host of players who ran Mosley out of bounds for a loss, forced the Aggies into a field goal attempt. David Hardy easily converted the 37-yard kick to give A&M an all-important seven-point lead, 17-10. BYU would now need a TD and two-point conversion to win. Only seven minutes remained.

The emotions of BYU fans had been yanked around like a yo-yo all night. And nothing illustrated this better than the next two plays. Homer Jones returned the kickoff after A&M's field goal all the way to midfield. Yo-yo up. Then Wilson, under pressure from A&M's ever-pestering defense, tossed his third interception of the night. Yo-yo down.

The Aggies now had a seven-point lead, the ball on their own 45-yard line, just over six minutes to play and a choir of 40,000 fans singing their praises. Within 45 seconds they also had a third down and less than a yard to go. Mosley tried to get the distance himself but was thwarted by the entire BYU defense, it seemed.

Fourth and inches. An A&M punt could well pin the Cougars deep in their own territory, a place they had not been able to drive from all night. But A&M Coach Wilson made a third strategic decision that backfired. He decided to go for the first down. Mosley fumbled the ball about even with the yardstick. But the world will never know if A&M got its first down. BYU, and more specifically defensive tackle Pulusila "Junior" Filiaga, had the ball.

BYU made the events of the final five minutes even more improbable by failing to get a first down after the big break. They still trailed by a touchdown, but the Cougars had field position — a valuable weapon, if they could just get a good punt off.

Brown satisfied Necessity No. 1 by dropping his kick at the A&M 4-yard line. This was just the first in a series of interlocking necessities.

Now BYU had to stop A&M, which had a running clock on its side. The offense that had burned the Cougars for more than 275 yards rushing couldn't even manage a first down. Necessity No. 2 had been fulfilled. Only 2:45 remained. The Cougars needed good field position again to have a realistic shot at a touchdown.

Tim Halverson, BYU's first improbable hero, took care of Necessity No. 3 by slipping around the right side of A&M's line and getting a big piece of David Appleby's punt. The ball rolled dead just 19 yards from where the Cougars wanted to end up — the A&M goal line. They certainly had field position!

It would have been nice if Necessity No. 4 — a touchdown — had come on a 19-yard pass on the first play. But it didn't, and BYU had to settle for bits and pieces of yardage, and even two gift penalties.

An offsides call gave BYU a first and five on the 14-yard line. Mike Lacey, the game's second improbable hero, slipped out of the backfield to catch a five-yard pass from Wilson. First and goal on the 9. Homer Jones, who led all BYU rushers with 53 yards, got a hard-earned yard to the 8. The clock continued to run down . . . 1:45 . . . 1:40 . . . Wilson's second-down pass attempt to Bill Davis was incomplete, but was quickly followed by a tell-tale yellow flag thrown almost on the spot where Davis tried to catch the pass. Pass interference it was, giving BYU a first down and goal again, this time from the 2.

Lacey burrowed into the left side of the line, only to be stopped for a one-yard loss. Second and goal . . . 1:15 . . . 1:05 . . . 1:00 . . . A Cougar specialty, the short pass, was called for second down. Tight end Clay Brown was to block the defender opposite him, then roll off the block and run just over the goal line. Ideally, the play would be run so quickly that the A&M pass rush wouldn't be able to get close to Wilson.

The appendix-less quarterback took the snap with 55 seconds left to play. The dropback was quick. Brown stood up the defender, then quickly tore away from him. It was about four steps to the end zone. None of the defensive backs picked him up. He turned to face Wilson. A pass was lobbed the short distance between the two. Brown had the ball

clutched against the blue No. 85 on his jersey a full
second before A&M defenders converged on him and
knocked him to the ground. The 12th man's low
roar had again escalated — this time to a loud gasp.

Perhaps the moral victory was achieved with
Brown's clutch TD catch and Wilson's toss. But the
Cougars were now just one completed pass (or run)
from a bonafide victory.

No, LaVell Edwards never considered taking the
tie a relatively safe point-after kick would probably
give him: "It would have been wrong for me to go
for the tie when the kids wanted a victory so badly. I
didn't think about it for a second."

The offensive unit, still giddy over scoring the
touchdown, became even more excited when it was
signaled to remain on the field. Timeout was called
and Wilson summoned to the sidelines.

The Cougar quarterback, Edwards and offensive
coordinator Doug Scovil began discussing how to
make the conversion a game-winning, not -losing,
play. Wilson suggested a fake draw roll pass, where
a handoff would be faked to halfback Homer Jones.
Then Wilson would roll out to the left and hit fullback Mike Lacey (the unlikely hero) in the end zone.

The coaches weren't convinced the play would
work. "I can see why," recalled Wilson. "The defense wouldn't be expecting a run on a conversion
play, so there's no need to fake one, especially a
draw."

But Wilson, who had overcome appendicitis and
a 102-degree temperature to reach this moment,
asserted, "I think it will be wide open." Edwards
and Scovil decided to listen to their quarterback
once more. A fake draw roll pass it would be.

As Wilson jogged back toward the huddle around
the 10-yard line, adjusting his flak jacket as he went,

A&M's 12th man began building an incredible wall of noise. The clamor seemed to grow second by second. An unsuspecting Lacey tugged at his helmet, now ringing from the enveloping noise, and leaned in to listen to Wilson's instructions.

Yes, the crowd was so loud it seemed that all 40,000 people were peering over his shoulder into the huddle. But Lacey wasn't hearing things — his number *had* just been called. BYU was resting its hopes on a converted linebacker not noted for his pass-catching abilities, but known rather as an intense competitor and a fine athlete. Wilson glanced at Lacey and patted him on the back. "Let's go," is all the quarterback told his team.

As Wilson walked up to the line of scrimmage, the crowd reached a clamorous zenith. But his attention was focused not on the crowd, but on the developing defense. "Aha!" The defender responsible for covering Lacey had lined up on the wrong side of the ball and would be out of position to pursue the quick play. As long as the defensive player stayed there, it would take a total breakdown to keep the Cougars out of the end zone. Wilson relaxed a little and bent down over the center.

Somehow Wilson's signal-calling voice was heard above the din. The ball was snapped quickly. The ill-placed defender hadn't moved! Wilson faked the handoff to Jones and began moving to his left. All was going well so far. But as Wilson readied to make the short throw, an A&M lineman moved in front of him, arms high above his nearly 6½-foot frame. Wilson's view of Lacey was blocked; he didn't have time to elude the massive obstacle. He had just one choice — he threw the ball just over the jumping defender, hoping his receiver would, somehow, find his way to it.

Lacey was open, but Wilson's delivery would be a

hard one to catch, even if he were the nimblest of wide receivers. In a split-second reaction, like slamming on a car's brakes, Lacey left his feet to dive for the ball that still seemed an eternity away. His body was almost parallel to the ground as his fingers met the leather oblong. He clutched it and tried to bring it into his body. It played pinball with his chest pads for an agonizing moment before he finally gathered it in and hit the turf. The referee sprinted to where Lacey lay, then thrust his arms high above his head.

As if a light had been turned off, the roaring 12th man let out a faint groan, then fell quiet. The 150-or-so cheering BYU followers in the stadium were swallowed up in the silence.

Lacey looked up and saw BYU's giant offensive linemen dancing above him. "Right then," he said, "it hit me. I realized exactly what I'd done." The Cougar celebration swirled around Lacey and followed him to the sidelines, where disbelieving teammates showered him with raucous congratulations, hearty backslaps and embraces.

But there was one small matter left to deal with — 52 seconds. Even a field goal, and A&M's David Hardy was capable of kicking a 50-yarder, would win the game for the Aggies. There was plenty of time for a drive to scoring territory.

Texas A&M started from its own 26-yard line and swept down the field to the BYU 34 before Hardy was hurried in to attempt his kick, a 51-yarder. The 12th man now sensed a remarkable A&M win in the offing and raised its Texas-sized voice once again.

The kick was launched from the steamy Rice Stadium turf, and, unlike the punt a few minutes earlier, no Cougar managed to lay even a finger on it. The ball was on its unhindered path toward the goal posts, which gaped, so it seemed to BYU's help-lessly watching players, as wide as nearby Galveston Bay. But wait! The kick was gradually fading to the left. It kept sliding . . . and sliding . . . and sliding . . .

The Cougar celebration, delayed by 48 seconds of added drama, suddenly erupted as the ball sailed just left of the goal posts.

Wilson and his offensive cohorts triumphantly paraded onto the field one last time. The quarter-back took the game's final snap and dropped to one knee. It was over.

Aggie fans filed out of Rice Stadium in disbelief. How could their team have lost? Their disbelief would turn to shock when reading the next morn-ing's newspaper. A&M had amassed 404 total yards to BYU's 217; it had controlled the ball for more than 35 of 60 minutes, and led for more than 50. And the Aggies had held one of the nation's top offenses to just 165 yards passing, harassed its quarterback all night and even intercepted three of his passes. They had done all this, yet still lost.

The shock waves from this stunning upset began to ripple outward across the country. In Provo, it was another New Year's celebration, as people in many parts of the city grabbed pots, pans and car horns to fill an otherwise calm September night with a spontaneous victory chime.

The BYU locker room was predictably chaotic. "Stonehands" Lacey, kick blocker Halverson and suddenly healthy Wilson were all saluted by team-mates. But the game ball was not given to any of these three—it would belong to fallen teammate Danny Frazier, who would soon be en route to Salt Lake City by special airplane to have his broken neck cared for. With this one symbol, BYU's biggest win ever was dedicated to Frazier.

Gifford Nielsen strolled into the Houston Oilers' pregame meal Sunday morning in the Pittsburgh Marriott and quickly scanned the room for a newspaper. He found one and tore into it, searching for the sports section. The headline "BYU Shocks Texas A&M" jumped up at him from one of the pages.

Nielsen gleefully passed the news to his teammates, pointing out to certain ones just which seafood dinner he planned on ordering from his favorite restaurant — Captain Benny's.

"BYU's football program suddenly gained a lot of respect among the Oilers that day," added the happy Nielsen.

The national press, slow to give the BYU football program respect, was quick to herald the upset. The Cougars jumped into 20th place in the following week's national rankings.

Gary Kama, who played what Coach Edwards called "as outstanding a game as any linebacker in BYU history," was named the Associated Press National Defensive Player of the Week. Edwards himself was chosen the United Press International's National Coach of the Week.

And the next issue of Sports Illustrated recited several upsets, but called BYU's felling of A&M the "biggest surprise" of them all.

Marc Wilson went on to lead his team to an unblemished 11-0 regular-season record — BYU's best ever. The Cougars led the nation in total offense, per-game passing and points scored. The No. 9 national ranking at regular season's end was the highest ever awarded the school. The nation had finally come to notice BYU football. And Wilson fulfilled predictions by being selected a consensus all-America and finishing third in voting for the Heisman Trophy.

But it all nearly ended with a Houston Friday Night Fever . . .

7

Second Time Around

Jim Jimas leans back against the bleacher seats, shaking his head. "I'm 39 years old. People still ask me about it. Not just around here, but everywhere I go. They still remember. I guess we didn't realize how big a deal it was. We knew winning the NIT was something special, but we didn't know it was that big. I didn't know it would affect us the rest of our lives. . . ."

It was still easy in 1966 to believe in dreams coming true. Unknown Texas Western was on its way to a national basketball championship. You could move across the country for a $2,000 raise and say you were living better. Gas was cheap and teenagers still dragged Main. The papers carried ads proclaiming the television news that night would be in living color. Gemini 8 was in space and man would soon walk on the moon.

But it was, too, the beginning of a turbulent time of transition as the innocence slipped away. The giddy optimism of the '50s and early '60s had begun to tarnish with the changing complexion of a nation. Kennedy had fallen to a sniper's gun just over two years earlier; his brother and Martin Luther King would shortly follow. Three men were found guilty in New York of the murder of Malcom X.

A half-page ad in the New York *Times* that March fervently screamed: "Stop this war now!"—a war few knew anything about except that it was taking young men to Southeast Asia to stop Communist aggression.

The Soviets were closing the arms gap. Campus unrest was beginning to stir. The Watts section of Los Angeles had burned angrily in the August heat seven months earlier and would again this week.

All was not right, but again, it was still just 1966 and, other than the fear of being drafted, the biggest concern to most college kids was getting enough gas in the Chevy to get to the drive-in.

Things weren't perfect, but people could still look the other way without closing their eyes. They could find other things to worry about and in New York City, if you liked basketball, you could worry about who would win the National Invitation Tournament.

It was a better way than most to sit out a week in March beneath the gray skies and towering corridors of Manhattan.

Brigham Young University had its most exciting basketball team ever that year. There had been other good ones, including the 1951 team that won the NIT, but none had set the blistering scoring pace of this one. Ten times the Cougars had scored over

100 points. Their fast-breaking, court-length passing offense had produced a startling 95.5 points a game.

There really wasn't much to say about the Cougars except they liked to run and shoot. They topped the 100-point mark in five of their first six games. Playing basketball was solid fun and Utah was making a case for itself as a basketball Mecca. The Cougars were in the NIT and the University of Utah would become one of the Final Four teams in the NCAA tournament.

BYU was a typical college team, complete with nicknames and practical jokes. The best at pinning labels on others was senior guard Jeff Congdon. He made up most of the names—"Ninety-eight percent of them, anyway," said a teammate—and they always seemed to fit painfully well. Six-foot-11 center Jim Eakins was "Bronto" and the other 6-foot-11 center, Craig Raymond, was "Stretch." No explanations needed there. The team's Dick Nemelka was called "Cyrano," as in de Bergerac, because of his prominent nose. He was described in *Sports Illustrated* as "a blond, flat-nosed 6-footer whose specialty is shooting."

Jimas was "Ringo" because of his resemblance to the Beatles heartthrob. Congdon, one of the few non-Mormons on the team when he arrived at BYU, was "Deacon." Assistant basketball coach Pete Witbeck was "Napoleon" because they considered him a little general. And head coach Stan Watts was "Abe" after Harlem Globetrotters' founder Abe Saperstein.

Watts's nickname had nothing to do with physical characteristics. It came about this way: before one regular season game the Cougars were going through their warmups and got more carried away than usual with behind-the-back passing, dribbling be-

tween the legs, twisting shots and a grand assort-
ment of showboat moves. BYU wound up losing the
contest, which irked Watts considerably. "You guys
think you're the Harlem Globetrotters out there!"
Watts chided. The next practice he made them shoot
an hour's worth of layups — minus the fancy moves.

Thus the nickname. If they were the Globetrotters, he was their leader.

If ever there was a BYU team tailor-made to win,
this was it. They had size — including three 6-11
players — strength, shooting ability and speed. Their
fast break was nationally recognized. Nemelka, a 53-
percent shooter who averaged 24 points a game,
made *Look* magazine's all-America team. BYU set a
school record to that date in field goal percentage,
hitting half its shots. There was even a rumor it was
a decent defensive team, though a team scoring
nearly 100 points every time it took the court had
little reason to worry about defense.

It was as well-balanced and deep a team as BYU
has ever assembled. At center it was normally Raymond, a junior, starting. Though more talented than
Eakins, the two were switched back and forth during
the year because the determined, hard-working, dis-
ciplined Eakins would earn the starting spot for
several games before Raymond would take the position back.

The forwards were Cedar City junior Neil Roberts
and Sandy senior Steve Kramer. Roberts was a tre-
mendous athlete, a decathlon star with great speed.
Kramer was the toughest player on the team. "Absolutely fearless," said one BYU official who watched
Kramer play that season.

The team's heart was its guards. Congdon and
Nemelka were a captivating pair, Congdon a phenomenal passer and the less flamboyant Nemelka

Defense wasn't something the Cougars had to play much of in 1966. Pictured are Jim Eakins (53), Dick Nemelka (20), Steve Kramer (33), Neil Roberts (31), and Jeff Congdon (23).

the top scorer with a brilliant outside shooting ability.

But what made the team so effective was its depth. Backing up the 6-foot-5 Roberts was 6-foot-4 junior Gary Hill, an all-around talent who was one of the most touted prep players ever in Utah. The third guard was Jimas, a smart, poised junior who slipped effortlessly into the lineup for Congdon or Nemelka, usually playing equally as well as either starter.

So they had a well-balanced starting lineup with a strong backup at all three positions.

And they had confidence. A whole lot of confidence.

When it came down to naming the starting lineup, Watts went with Craig Raymond (left) for the final game against NYU.

The guardline was deep in talent in 1966, with the likes of Dick Nemelka (left) and Jim Jimas.

The combination was devastating. BYU went 17-5 through the regular season, 20-5 overall. The Cougars won every home game for the second year in a row.

When St. Joseph's arrived in Provo ranked No. 2 in the nation, BYU won by a whopping 20 points and was ranked in the Top 10. The St. Joseph's players had been so confident of beating BYU they had vowed to walk home if they lost. Not only did they lose, but the game was televised along the Eastern seaboard to millions of surprised viewers.

The Cougars pounded Illinois. They crushed Houston. They even beat nationally ranked Utah not once, but twice, including a one-pointer in Salt Lake City. The way they had it figured, if they were running they were winning, and they were doing plenty of both.

BYU's confidence was not necessarily born in the early season, but during a summer trip to South America. The Cougars played 22 games, winning 19, and the trip brought them together in a way no domestic trip could. During a game in Uruguay Raymond elbowed an opponent who happened to be a star on their Olympic team. They needed a police escort to leave the arena afterwards.

After winning the first six games of the year, BYU moved to Philadelphia for the Quaker City Tournament. The Cougars were nationally ranked and their reputation preceded them. One newspaper described BYU's attack as "Two dribbles, a 40-foot pass and a 30-foot shot."

And, as it was duly recorded, most of the 30-foot shots went in.

But, to the Cougars' consternation, in Philadelphia they suffered their first loss of the year, falling 71-69 to LaSalle. They were surprised not only that LaSalle could beat them, but that anybody could beat them—they had been playing so tremendously. BYU came back, however, to beat St. Bonaventure and Cornell in the other tournament games.

Western Athletic Conference games followed, with BYU stepping on Arizona and Arizona State. However, the Cougars quickly followed with road losses to New Mexico and Wyoming. Utah and BYU went through the conference season fighting for the lead until the Provo team lost two games in Arizona on the next-to-last week of the season. Though the Cougars won their final three conference games over New Mexico, Wyoming and Utah, they had forfeited their conference chances on the Arizona trip. BYU finished 6-4 in the WAC and Utah won the title with a 7-3 record.

Utah entered the NCAA tournament as the WAC representative and BYU, not unknown in the East due to the success against St. Joseph's and appearance at the Quaker City Tournament, entered the NIT as the No. 1 seed.

Thus, the Cougars headed East, fully expecting to win the NIT. Despite the loss of starter Neil Roberts to an injury the last game of the regular season, there was always, always the confidence that permeated the team. Though they knew Roberts would be missed, they were certain they would not be stopped by his injury. Teammates were more concerned, it seemed, about Roberts missing the upcoming track and field season than not having him for the NIT. He was good, but so was Gary Hill and he would fill the position adequately.

BYU figured itself a team of destiny. Last time a Cougar team had gone to South America, in 1951, it won the NIT. They were anxious to prove themselves to a rather skeptical New York press and public and, unlike the 1951 event, this one would have the advantage of national television coverage.

On the merits of its seeding BYU drew a bye the first round, leaving Saturday morning, March 12, for New York. Shortly after arriving the Cougars sought some court time for practice but were unable to get on the Garden floor. They didn't practice on Sunday, leaving only a short Monday afternoon shoot-around before they faced their first opponent, Temple. The Owls had gotten to the quarterfinals with a win over Virginia Tech the week before.

BYU's plan to win the tournament notwithstanding, there was considerable concern over Temple. It had the size and talent to match up with the Cougars well. The Owls were led by 6-foot-8 center Jim Williams and 6-foot-4 Ken Morgan and 6-foot-7 Clarence Brookins at forwards. "I'm always worried about that first game in a big city," Watts told George Ferguson of the *Deseret News.* "The kids, especially the inexperienced and younger ones, are wide-eyed at it all and in sort of a daze when that first whistle blows."

But if anyone was in a daze at the game's start it was Temple, all agog in the early moments at BYU's run-and-gun assault. It took BYU only eight seconds to score its first basket and in just over three minutes the Cougars had an 8-0 lead.

Temple recovered quickly, Williams and Brookins pouring in points until the Owls had the lead, 24-22 midway through the half. BYU emerged from the halftime locker room trailing by two, only to watch Morgan score seven straight Owl points early in the second half for a 51-47 lead. BYU settled in, taking a 56-54 lead with 12:30 left in the half, and the Cougars never trailed again, gradually extending the lead to the final 90-78 margin.

While Nemelka got 27 and Congdon 22, only in

the second half did BYU return to its pace of the early going. Despite Williams' 38-point, 20-rebound performance, BYU's depth paid off as four players scored in double figures, including 18 for Kramer and 10 for Eakins. A profusion of Temple turnovers — seven in the last 10 minutes — kept the Owls from seriously threatening in the late game.

Meanwhile, No. 2 seed Wichita lost its first game to New York University, the team that would eventually meet the Cougars in the finals. An Army upset over favored San Francisco set the BYU squad up against a deliberate, plodding Cadet team — a team without much size and limited talent, and a volatile 25-year-old first-year coach who said what he thought and usually got in trouble for it. His name was Bobby Knight.

Watts had been quoted in the press as having wanted to meet Army rather than the taller San Francisco in the semifinals. Though Army had the least talent of any team BYU met in the tournament, it presented the most opposition. It was a stark contrast in styles, the frantic BYU offense matching up against Army's deliberate, physical, methodical style.

Thursday night 18,499 fans, including a large body of Cadets, pushed into Madison Square Garden for the semifinals. Army entered the game 18-6, its hopes of a brilliant season shaken when 6-foot-6, 250-pound all-America candidate Mike Sillman went down with an injury in January.

Army's lineup, greatly outsized by BYU, had only 6-foot-5 sophomore Mike Noonan to match up with BYU's big inside players. The most dangerous player was 6-foot-3 Bill Helkie who had scored 26 points early in the year to hand New York University its first loss of the season.

From the start it was a jarring, sometimes mean-spirited game, BYU astounded at the amount of contact allowed by the officials. Though obviously outmatched, Army took a 25-12 lead in the early going behind Helkie's outside shooting and held on to lead 31-24 at half time.

The second half was more of the same: pushing and elbowing, with BYU unable to play its wide-open game well. An early second-half rally in which the Cougars outscored Army 17-10 tied the score at 41-41. The battle continued; at one point Kramer was knocked out when he landed on his jaw, only to arise and return to the fray. Neither team was able to gain a lasting lead as the game moved into its final frantic minutes.

Helkie, the Army star, fouled out with the scored tied and 2:17 remaining, sending Knight into a rage over the call. Jimas, who had spent considerable time on the bench during the game calculating how best to play against the rough servicemen, told the coaches he knew how to beat their opponent.

And indeed he did.

Eakins had fouled out and Watts, in an uncharacteristic move, had put Jimas in with Nemelka and Congdon for a three-guard look. Jimas stole the ball from Army guard Dick Murray, sweeping it away from the blind side and driving the length of the court for the layup, giving BYU a 60-58 lead with 1:45 left. "I remember the jubilation when he stole the ball," Eakins recalls. "There was this sigh of relief and yet this frustration that we had let ourselves get in that situation."

Raymond hit Jimas on a short driving shot and BYU led by four. BYU followed with a rebound shot and a pair of free throws, winning the game 66-60.

Afterwards Knight went berserk, kicking lockers and blaming the officials. It was to no avail. BYU had made it to the finals against hometown favorite NYU.

It was raining steadily in the gray morning light when Knight knocked on Watts's and Witbeck's door at the Taft Hotel at just after six. Knight's raincoat was damp as he stood in the hallway. Witbeck answered the door, letting Knight step in.

"Mr. Watts, can I talk to you?"

Watts said, "Of course," finding a chair for Knight.

"I want to apologize," Knight began, saying he had great respect for Watts and his program. He felt bad for sounding off after the game the night before, explaining that he was young and impetuous and asking for Watts' forgiveness.

Watts put his arm around Knight and smiled. "I understand," he said. "I was a young coach once, too. I want you to know you're going to be one of the bright young coaches in the country and it's just a matter of time until you win a national championship."

But this time, and in this tournament, the championship belonged only to Watts.

They had grown restless by Friday night, although the days had slipped by quickly, filled with press conferences and practices and hotel-room schoolwork. They had seen the Empire State Building and Broadway and the Statue of Liberty. Some had spent their spare time with books, others gathered in small, laughing groups to play Hearts. A few ventured out into the curious New York street life to stare at strange shops and stranger people.

If New York amazed the young BYU players, they were a rather unusual commodity to New York, too.

Not that an all-white basketball team was unheard of in 1966. Rather, it was their wide-open game as well as their determination to represent the Church well that attracted considerable press attention.

Even the flag girls and cheerleaders were publicized. A relatively young broadcaster by the name of Cosell did a piece on them. A flag twirler said they were approached by a Playboy Club representative and offered jobs. A New York newspaper columnist devoted an entire article to the cheerleaders, calling them "clear-skinned girls . . . with hair glistening as it falls to supple shoulders. . . ."

And continuing . . . "They have an abiding faith in their beliefs, these strong, eager young women of the West. They exhibit a poise, a surety of purpose in the sense of ideals not too often found in the effete East. . . ."

But BYU wasn't the only Mormon draw in town. The night before the championship game, West Jordan's Don Fullmer fought middleweight Jose Gonzalez in hopes that a win would bring him a title bout. He got neither, losing by a decision.

Nemelka, though, was the biggest BYU draw. He had scored 22 against St. Joseph's and 40 and 38 points on consecutive nights during the Quaker City tournament, enhancing his image with the eastern media.

Though BYU was favored from the start to win the NIT and a four-point favorite on game day to beat NYU, there were many who felt the home court would weigh heavily in NYU's favor. Several writers picked the Violets in a close one; others merely pointed out that NYU was playing before over 18,000 hometown fans. But Watts and his team weren't hearing any of it. "We haven't played our best basketball yet in the NIT," Nemelka told a writer after the Army game.

Most intriguing in the matchups was that between NYU guard Mal Graham, easily the Violets' best player, and Nemelka. Graham was an outstanding shooter and often ran off points in torrid streaks of brilliance. Watts warned his team in the pregame locker room not to let him get off to a big start.

After that things were less even. At a forward for NYU was gifted Stan McKenzie, a 22-point scorer who had the thankless chore of guarding whichever 6-11 center BYU chose to use. Other front-line starters were 6-foot-4 Bruce Kaplan and Charlie Silen to match up with BYU's similarly sized Steve Kramer and Gary Hill. While Congdon was to guard Graham it was Nemelka's job to stop 6-foot-3 guard Richie Dyer, whose ankle injury limited his scoring during the year.

Even so, the *World-Telegram* echoed the sentiments of many with this pick: "If this game were anywhere else we'd pick Brigham Young. But this is the Garden — where Violets bloom. NYU, 82-80."

On Saturday it began to dawn on the BYU players that they were on the verge of a major step in the school's sports history. They had fully expected to win when they arrived in New York, but the realization they were in the finals sobered them.

At 10:00 A.M. they began the pregame ritual they knew by rote. At mealtime, it was the same pregame menu as always: steak, baked potato, green beans, tossed salad and orange juice. While the meal was the same as usual, their guests weren't, as they were joined by actor Peter Falk and musician Mitch Miller for breakfast.

As the Cougars warmed up on the court, dimly lit by today's more modern arena standards, they were surprised to find that they were not total villains to the crowd. Aside from a number of LDS fans there was a sizable—perhaps 2,500 strong—number of Army cadets who, for some strange reason, had taken up the charge to cheer for BYU even though the Cougars had beaten Army two nights earlier.

Warmups ended and the teams moved to their dressing rooms for final instructions. Watts reminded his players that, despite NYU's 18-9 record and somewhat checkered success that year, the Violets could play exceptionally well. He warned them to watch Graham and keep McKenzie off the boards. "But the seniors especially were so confident," Eakins would remember 18 years later, "it was like a WAC game for them. The coach had to warn us not to overlook them."

There was one thing left to do: name the lineup.

Watts always waited until the closing moments before announcing his starters. Most of it was understood. Hill would start at forward with Roberts injured, as he had all tournament. He called out the other names: Nemelka, Congdon, Kramer . . .

He turned to Raymond. The big Vancouver, Washington, kid had not started for several games, but Watts didn't blink. "Craig, I'm gonna start you," he said. "I don't know why, but I have a feeling."

And a great feeling it was.

The game started at a blinding pace. Kaplan hit a jumper out front for the game's first points but 13 seconds later Raymond, who would have one of the great days of his career, stuffed a rebound to tie the score.

BYU showed no nervousness and little patience for waiting out the opponent. The Cougars quickly went ahead 13-8, appearing at first too much for the smaller Violets to handle.

Though BYU was hitting at better than a 50 percent clip, NYU couldn't be shaken and shot nearly as well. The Violets closed BYU's lead to a tie, locking things into a tight contest that was tied seven times before intermission.

Trouble, meanwhile, was brooding for the Cougars. Nemelka was in foul trouble from the first tip, picking up his first foul on a charge less than four minutes into the game. Two minutes later he got his second offensive foul, and when he picked up his third foul with only nine minutes gone in the game a wave of anticipation went through the crowd that he would be benched.

Nemelka looked at the bench. Watts only looked back, not moving.

"That's the first time I'd ever done that in my life," Watts remembers with a wan smile. "I always pulled a kid on the third foul."

Almost always.

Nemelka went past Watts, assuring him, "Don't worry, I'll be all right. I'll be careful."

But he picked up his fourth foul with BYU leading 42-40 and the first half not yet over. Jimas entered and Nemelka, disgusted at himself, plopped down next to Watts on the bench.

Even with Nemelka's troubles, BYU had remained in control through the first half, holding a 48-43 lead at intermission. NYU had no way of stopping the Cougar front line as Raymond scored 14 points and took down nine rebounds; Hill had 11 points, five rebounds and Kramer nine rebounds and eight points. BYU had shot a sterling 59 percent from the field.

Still, there was no way to shrug off the concern over Nemelka's foul woes. As the second half started, with Jimas still in the lineup, the coaches looked anxiously from the court to the clock, wishing the time would go faster. Jimas, meanwhile, showed no signs of nervousness as the Cougars outscored the

Violets 25-14 the first eight minutes. When the early offense didn't produce quick scoring, the big inside men took care of the points, working the area around the hoop with little opposition.

As NYU began to tire of losing out on the rebounding war, it became harder to get back against the Cougar fast break and the lead jumped to 18.

So far, though, NYU had managed to stay close enough to remain a threat, quietly cutting back the lead to within striking distance. But the Violets' final gasp for survival ended on the most spectacular play of the game with 6:40 left. Congdon brought the crowd to its feet by taking the ball off the dribble and slinging a one-handed, behind-the-head pass the length of the court to Hill, nobody within 40 feet of him. The throw had come with such quickness and accuracy that not only NYU, but Hill himself, was startled.

He threw the ball into the side of the iron before rebounding and putting it back in. "Aw, I just wanted to miss so I could make it more exciting," he told his teammates.

So impressed with Congdon's pass was Boston Celtics' coach Red Auerbach, who had been sitting four rows behind the BYU bench scouting for pro prospects, that he bolted to the BYU bench where Witbeck and Watts sat, swatting each on the back. "Hey, Stan! Pete! Did you see that pass? Did you see that pass!?"

Indeed he had, several times, in fact. Though the Cougar coach had been impressed with the play, he wasn't surprised, having caught Congdon's act for four years. He turned quickly to Auerbach, long enough to reply: "Yeah, Red, I saw it. I haven't got my eyes closed down here."

After the pass it was just waiting out the clock. NYU managed to get within ten points with 4:24 left, but BYU never let it get closer. Raymond finished with phenomenal stats — 21 points, 18 rebounds — an accomplishment made even more impressive when the center told reporters after the game that he got so nervous he "was about ready to throw up" when told he was starting the contest. Hill, the fill-in for Roberts, ended with 21 points and eleven boards and Kramer 20 points and nine rebounds.

NYU's McKenzie had led his team with 27 points while Graham scored 18 points, 14 in the first half.

Meanwhile Nemelka, who had sat on the bench since getting his fourth foul during the first half, finally returned with 5:56 to go and the Cougars clearly in charge. In a huddle during a timeout Jimas had suggested Nemelka spend the final moments of his career on the court, not the bench, so the two switched places. BYU finished with a 97-84 win.

Congdon and Nemelka cut the nets down in the Garden as Watts and Witbeck were lifted on the players' shoulders. Then they noisily crowded into the locker room while Watts headed to his nationally televised interview to explain how his team had earned the NIT title.

In Utah it was proclaimed the most prestigious sports accomplishment in the school's history, enhanced even more by the television coverage that wasn't available when BYU won the NIT in 1951. Watts, who had taken the Cougars to the first NIT title, too, told a reporter with a laugh, "It seemed easier, for some reason," the first time.

There were undoubtedly times during the 1966

tournament when Watts wondered if his team could repeat as champions in their fourth NIT appearance. But the players had expected nothing less.

The only thing they didn't expect was to be remembered for it so many years later.

8

It Was Quite a Show (Me)

Missouri Congressman William Duncan Vandiver stepped to the podium at an 1899 Philadelphia naval banquet. He then, legend has it, made the famous statement that typifies the dogged persistence and obstinacy of Missourians from Kansas City to St. Louis:

"I come from a state that raises corn and cotton and cockle-burrs and Democrats, and frothy eloquence neither convinces nor satisfies me. I am from Missouri. You have got to *show me.*"

Vandiver hailed from Columbia, a small city in the heart of the "Show-Me State." Along with cockle-burrs and Democrats, Columbia is also home of the University of Missouri.

Latter-day Saint Church leader Brigham Young, ailing and confined to the back of a wagon, asked to be propped up so he could better see the desolate valley of the Great Salt Lake below. He then, legend has it, made the famous statement that typifies the resourcefulness and cheery optimism of Utahns from Logan to St. George:

"It is enough. This is the right place. Drive on."

President Young and his pioneer followers went on to build up Salt Lake City and a host of other settlements in the region, among them Provo, a small city in the heart of the "Beehive State." Along with resourcefulness and cheery optimism, Provo is also home of Brigham Young's very own university.

When the University of Missouri football team learned it had been invited to the sixth Holiday Bowl, kicker Brad Burditt's reaction in the true spirit of William Duncan Vandiver, was (according to a Kansas City *Times* report), "*Where* is it?"

And the ol' show-me congressman must have done cartwheels in his grave to hear running back Eric Drain add, "No — *what* is it?"

The Brigham Young University football team, for the sixth straight year, had also earned a trip to the Holiday Bowl, due to its Western Athletic Conference championship. In the true spirit of Brigham Young, team members and coaches expressed not dismay, but sincere gratitude for the annual pilgrimage.

And Brother Brigham must have busted his buttons with pride, for when it was suggested that BYU, with its lofty national status (No. 9 ranking), had outgrown San Diego's fledgling post-season bowl, the invariable answer was a quick denial: there was *nowhere* the BYU team would rather be going than San Diego.

The honorable Mr. Vandiver would have been right proud of his hometown college's 1983 football squad. Though only 53 percent Missouri natives, it was led by fiery Warren Powers, a true Missourian by birth and temperament. A genuine show-me spirit permeated the group. Despite impressive physical ability, the team had produced a so-so 7-4 record. But it was Top 10 in self-confidence, 11-0 in games it felt it had really won.

Mizzou had its point. Were it not for an eerie tendency to self-destruct at the worst possible moment, it, not Nebraska, would have won the privilege of losing to Miami in the Orange Bowl.

Consider:

— Two fumbled punts inside Missouri's own 20-yard line handed Wisconsin a pair of easy touchdowns. A late Mizzou score could have won the game, but a two-point conversion failed. Wisconsin won 21-20, despite being outgained 366-175 in total yardage.

— A 34-yard touchdown pass from Marlon Adler to Greg Krahl was called back— Adler was across the line of scrimmage when passing. The TD would have at least tied East Carolina, which won 13-6.

— Top-ranked Nebraska led just 20-13 late in the third quarter when the Tigers drove twice within the Cornhusker 10-yard line. A fourth-and-inches on the 9 failed the first time, and Nebraska recovered a fumbled snap on the 1 the second time. The Huskers went on to win 34-13 in a game that was statistically even.

— A pair of pass interceptions in the end zone and a fumble stopped fourth-quarter drives against Kansas. The Jayhawks won 37-27, but were again outdone in total yardage by Mizzou.

To these losses, add victories over such foes as Big 10 champion Illinois, Oklahoma (a shutout) and bowl-bound Oklahoma State and maybe you can understand why the Missouri team felt no one all season really did "show me."

The young Tigers (twice as many underclassmen as seniors and juniors) had already exceeded all expectations. Picked fifth in the tough Big 8, they instead tied for second with Oklahoma. (Second would have been theirs alone had they beaten Kansas.)

But that wasn't good enough. The Tigers viewed themselves among the top teams in the nation, better than their record showed, and were miffed at their unranked status.

An invitation to a bowl some said they'd never heard of wasn't their idea of proper recognition. When reminded that their opponent would be No. 9 Brigham Young, a squad that executed the pass even better than Kansas (which had just shredded their secondary for 354 yards), Tigers assured everyone that their one-time lapse wouldn't be repeated. (At least they didn't go into their "Where's Brigham Young, no *what's* Brigham Young?" routine again.)

The official word from Missouri was that the players' indignation at stooping to the Holiday Bowl was quieted once they sat down and watched BYU game films—that they now respected their foe and, thus, the bowl they'd meet them in.

If you believe that, after what you'll read in this chapter, you will also believe that Utah freely sprouts cotton, cockle-burrs . . . and Democrats.

The honorable President Young would have been right proud of his namesake college's 1983 football squad. Though only 35 percent Utah natives, it was led by mild-mannered LaVell Edwards, a true Utahn by birth and temperament. A genuine Beehive State spirit permeated the group.

That spirit found a literal embodiment in quarterback Steve Young, a lineal descendant of Brigham himself. Yes, he was cheerily optimistic, and oh, my, was he resourceful!

BYU's offensive philosophy, in a nutshell, was to pass, but only in chunks the defense was willing to yield. That philosophy had never found a better executor than Young. "The most accurate arm in NCAA history, with a Tom Landry mind," wrote the Kansas City *Times'* Tom Shatel.

If the defense allowed long passes, Young could zip it downfield with the best of them. If it didn't, he had the patience to hit receivers on short patterns or even dump off to running backs out of the backfield. If everyone was covered, he could tuck the ball under his arm and run with the speed and effectiveness of most halfbacks.

If Young sounds too good to be true, that's what most opposing coaches thought after playing against him. He completed an unheard-of 71.3 percent of his passes (an all-time record), including 22 in a row once (also a record), and racked up total offense averaging 395 yards per game (another record).

Some people thought he was the best college player in the country, and were it not for Nebraska's Mike Rozier's record-shattering season, he probably would have easily won the Heisman Trophy. He finished second to Rozier in the balloting. (An Associated Press report showed how Young felt about the whole thing: "I don't know if I'm the best guy in my own locker room, and you're talking about the nation.")

And wait, that's not all. Young could also turn and hand the ball to a trio of running backs who averaged a whopping *seven* yards a carry between them — all season! If this offense sounds too good to be true, that's also what most opposing coaches thought after trying to defend against it. As for moving the ball, college football had never produced a more unstoppable force. Its 584.2 yards per game was an all-time NCAA record. Most yards came via the pass, but, incredibly, the Cougars were also ranked No. 31 in the nation in rushing. A 10-1 record was the product, and the offense scored 36 points in the single loss.

Unstoppable? Teams usually tried to slow the BYU attack in two ways: either pressure the quarterback through blitzes or other rushing stunts, or drop back extra defenders into the secondary for pass coverage. Here are examples of how those approaches fared.

Teams that pressured the BYU quarterback:

New Mexico — Young was 24 of 30 (80 percent) in passing for 340 yards, four touchdowns. The team rushed for 270 yards, set a new Western Athletic Conference record with 777 yards total offense and scored 66 points.

Bowling Green — Young was 30 of 40 (75 percent) for 384 yards, five touchdowns. The team rushed for 192 yards, compiled 33 first downs and scored 63 points.

Wyoming — Young completed 23 of 39 (59 percent) for 356 yards, two touchdowns. The team rushed for 228 yards and scored 41 points.

And teams that dropped defenders back:

Air Force — Young was 39 of 49 (80 percent) for 486 yards, three touchdowns. The team rushed for 229 yards, broke a school record with 39 first downs and scored 46 points.

UCLA — Young completed 25 of 36 (69 percent) for 270 yards, two touchdowns. The team rushed for 265 yards, rang up 34 first downs and scored 37 points.

Utah — Young connected on 22 of 25 (88 percent) for 268 yards, six touchdowns. The team added 238 rushing yards and scored 55 points.

The Cougars were a seasoned team that still surpassed all expectations, particularly on offense. They won the WAC title, as anticipated, for the eighth straight year. After the opening loss to Baylor (which also went to a bowl game), BYU climbed steadily in the national polls, peaking at No. 9 at the end of the season.

That was just fine with the Cougars. And though some fans contended a second-place finish in the WAC would actually land the team in a more prestigious post-season game, no one officially connected with BYU ever publicly expressed less than total satisfaction with another trip to the Holiday Bowl.

And when some of those same boosters complained that Missouri (like 7-4 Indiana in 1979) wasn't a worthy opponent for the ninth-ranked team in the nation, BYU was quick to defend the Tigers. Edwards (who graciously builds up foes his team eventually beats 55-7) began likening Missouri to Ohio State, who had routed his Cougars 47-17 in the previous Holiday Bowl, a comparison even Kansas City-area writers said was far overgenerous. Nevertheless, Edwards said, his Cougars knew they had a dangerous foe on their hands, one worthy of everyone's respect.

If BYU didn't respect Missouri, after what you will read in this chapter, then the beehive might become Missouri's new helmet insignia.

William Duncan Vandiver wouldn't have hired LaVell Edwards to be his head football coach, no siree. So when the BYU mentor flew to Columbia after the 1977 season to interview for the Missouri post vacated by Al Onofrio, is it any wonder that Vandiver's spiritual descendants had already made up their minds, that they had already decided on Warren Powers, a former Nebraska assistant, head coach of one year at Washington State . . . and Missouri native?

LaVell Edwards, a true Utahn, at Missouri? They'd have driven him right out of the state. Or would he have fled first?

Actually, this Missouri-BYU matchup held more intrigue than many Tiger players and Cougar fans thought. The unheralded Holiday Bowl pitted teams that had beaten Illinois and UCLA, who would make several times as much money a week hence in the Rose Bowl.

Mizzou's opening-week victory over the Illini at Columbia had been convincing. The Tigers jumped to a 21-0 lead in the first half before settling for a 28-18 final margin. Missouri's defense caused six turnovers and allowed just 35 yards rushing all game.

BYU's verdict over the Bruins, 37-35, had also been convincing—at least offensively. Were it not for BYU's porous pass defense, allowing a big UCLA comeback, the game would have been a rout. The Cougars rolled up 535 yards total offense in incredibly balanced fashion—265 on the ground and 270 through the air.

And they could compare notes over a common opponent. Missouri had survived a late Utah State rally to hang on for a 17-10 win over the Aggies. USU quarterback Chico Canales burned Mizzou's defense for 166 yards passing in the fourth quarter and almost pulled out the game. But the Aggies couldn't budge the ball on the ground, netting just 54 yards, and their offense before the fourth quarter was poor. Missouri called 60 running plays and just 14 passes, grinding out 256 yards on the ground.

And it took a final-minute touchdown by Steve Young to resurrect a 38-34 BYU victory over Utah

State several weeks later. The Cougars dominated statistically, but could never shake the Aggies on the scoreboard. BYU's defense allowed 338 yards total offense (a better-than-average performance for them), but the offense piled up 527 yards, 359 through the air.

If you are getting the feel of a classic defense vs. offense and power running vs. wide-open passing confrontation, you're on the right track. Yes, yes, you're right. The Ohio State-BYU matchup of a year before was supposed to provide the same appeal, with far-from-appealing results. But Missouri vs. BYU had an extra dimension that made it even more potentially interesting than BYU-OSU: also competing, it would become apparent, was the spirit of William Duncan Vandiver against the spirit of Brigham Young.

No, this isn't a simple melodrama where heroes are always heroic and villains always villainous. Not everyone from Missouri mocked the Holiday Bowl and BYU, and not everyone from BYU showed due respect for Missouri. For that matter, not everyone from Missouri is doggedly persistent and obstinate, and not everyone from Utah is resourceful and cheerily optimistic.

But there were rather distinct vibes — karma, if you will — emanating from these two teams during the week leading to the Holiday Bowl.

Missouri players did, in interviews, give their opponent more credit than before. But "off camera," they frequently taunted, mocked and heckled Cougar players. And, in a particularly ugly incident, defensive back Kyle Morrell reports that as BYU was trotting into the stadium tunnel after practice, tobacco juice and spit rained down from Missouri players leaning over the exit.

It was called intimidation. Ohio State had practiced it the previous year, hadn't they? One difference, says defensive captain Todd Shell: "Ohio State
was a classy team. They treated us decently off the
field and were determined to show us on the field."

And lest you think Mizzou players arrived at
their evaluation of BYU by osmosis, consider the
team's coaches. While some were heaping lavish
praise on BYU, and Steve Young in particular, other
coaches were, as reported by Doug Robinson in the
Deseret News, driving into a gas station and openly
boasting that they'd handle BYU with no trouble.

"It was obvious from the start," says one BYU
coach, "that even though we were the ranked team,
they felt they were superior to us. You could sense
it. And our players consistently said that about their
contact with Missouri players."

Meanwhile, LaVell Edwards persisted in com-
paring Missouri to Ohio State, lauding its size, speed
and athletic ability. BYU players, while confident
they were on the better team, gave the Tigers their
due almost without exception.

But the message from Missouri was clear: Show
me.

Show me. When would the BYU football program
ever have to stop showing me? *It* was the team rated
ninth-best in the entire nation. And yet *it* was the
team, not Missouri, with something to prove.

BYU had compiled one of the country's best
records over the previous several years. But that performance, critics claimed, was cheapened by a weak
schedule and membership in a weak league (logic
akin to the notion that enrollment at Harvard auto-
matically makes one a genius.)

So BYU upgraded its schedule and began playing
creditably well against some in college football's

upper echelon. Then zap—one 30-point loss to Ohio State and the cries arose: "Aha, didn't we tell you? BYU can't play with the big boys."

The Cougars are still looked at as orphans in the Top 20. No one questions that an 8-3 Michigan can be the No. 9 team in the nation, but a 10-1 BYU in that spot? With reservations. Perhaps an asterisk should accompany the ranking with the caution: "We're not sure about this one."

That's why as the season progresses, and as BYU adds win upon win, you can visualize the voters covering their eyes and reluctantly granting the Cougars an obligatory ranking, realizing that they have to put a 6-1 team in there somewhere, since 4-2 teams are also ranked. But no, they don't belong up there with the rest of the 6-1 teams, the *traditional power* 6-1 teams. They belong several places back, with the faltering powers and up-and-coming, surprise, Cinderella teams. BYU's 55-7 win over Colorado State is different from Nebraska's 55-7 win over Kansas State, because Kansas State is, well, in the Big 8.

And you can follow the logic all the way through. Since the WAC is not as strong as the Big 8, that means the best team in the WAC must be about as good as the third- or fourth-best team from the Big 8. They really believe it, too. Why else would unranked Missouri consider itself superior to ninth-ranked BYU?

Yes, the pressure *was* on BYU. It had to show not only Missouri, but a nationwide football establishment that still didn't believe it was *that* good.

Cougars fans looking for omens as they sat in Jack Murphy Stadium just before Friday's 6:00 P.M. kickoff were getting mixed ones. The only coach in the United States who had played both BYU and

Missouri that season was contacted by Provo's *Daily Herald*. Utah State coach Chris Pella predicted the Cougars would "score more than 20 points and win by just a few."

Another good omen: the BYU basketball team had just won. The Cougar football squad had taken two Holiday Bowls following BYU basketball wins earlier the same evening. The Cougar cagers had played Boise State at the Marriott Center in a rare weekday afternoon game and, though given a tougher game than expected, managed to win 66-54.

On the other hand, as much as Steve Young wanted to change it this night, the fact remained that Jim McMahon was the only quarterback who had ever won bowl games for BYU—twice in seven attempts.

And history buffs had to be dismayed with the similarity between Missouri and BYU's 1979 Holiday Bowl opponent—Indiana. Both teams were 7-4, underrated and generally unwelcome as an opponent by BYU fans. Both teams faced a ninth-ranked Cougar squad. Both came from traditionally strong, proud conferences. Both wanted to end BYU winning streaks stretching into double digits.

Indiana beat BYU 38-37.

An omen connected to William Duncan Vandiver or Brigham Young couldn't be found. Their part in the game would just have to be settled on the field.

Defense was the key to winning this game; both head coaches said as much. The much-analyzed idiosyncrasies of both teams didn't amount to much alongside Mizzou defensive end Taft Sales's assessment, as reported in the *Deseret News*: "BYU can't stay with us physically."

If the Cougars could, they'd win the game. If they couldn't, they'd lose.

It took less than four minutes to establish the tone of Holiday Bowl VI. Missouri's first six plays were runs. BYU's defense, invited to rise to the occasion by Mizzou's outlook on the game, showed it wouldn't yield yardage at will. BYU's first play was a pass. Tiger defensive end Bobby Bell, son of Kansas City Chiefs' ex-great Bobby Bell, Sr., blew past the Cougar offensive line to sack Steve Young for a loss of eight yards. And both teams were emotionally in the ionosphere.

But things took an unexpected, and unwanted, tumble for BYU. On the third play from scrimmage, Young, again pursued by Bell and his defensive cohorts, threw a pass easily intercepted by cornerback Jerome Caver. Just eight running plays and 43 yards later, Eric Drain powered up the middle for a two-yard touchdown run. Though BYU had looked tough in its first defensive series, the Tigers rammed the ball downfield this time with distressing ease. A half quarter had passed and the Tigers led 7-0. They were also, as Sales had predicted, physically dominating the Cougars.

BYU's offense showed a few signs of life in its second possession. Young started connecting on short passes and took off on a 22-yard jaunt himself when all the receivers were covered. But once the Cougars crossed the 50-yard line, things changed. Bell, assisted by linebacker Tracey Mack, sacked Young for the second time. Then Bell took hold of Young's jersey for a third sack, but the Y quarterback managed to escape. Young probably would have preferred getting the sack, for he rolled right and threw, off-balance, downfield toward wide re-

ceiver Glen Kozlowski. Tiger free safety Reco Hawkins tipped the ball and it was scooped up by Sales
before hitting the grass.

Missouri had already ground out a scoring drive
against the BYU defense. And now the one thing
Cougar fans thought they could count on, the offense, was misfiring.

BYU then stopped Missouri without a first down,
but only a great *defensive* effort by Cougar wide
receiver Adam Haysbert prevented Jerome Caver
from getting his second interception, and Missouri
its third.

The first quarter ended with the Cougars down
7-0, and somewhat disoriented. The defense was
playing quite well, but so was Missouri's. BYU receiver coach Norm Chow, calling offensive plays
from the press box high above the field, knew something had to be done. "We knew Missouri would be a
good team, but they were even better than they
appeared on film. It was unbelievable the way they
were reacting to our plays."

It's not unusual for a precision-execution team
like BYU to look sour at first after a long layoff, but
Young's errant passing would soon dig the Cougar
defense a hole it couldn't escape from.

Chow would have to figure a way to get the offense moving. But for now, another coach in the
booth had the game in his hands. Defensive coordinator Dick Felt's squad would have to stop the
Tigers at least one more time.

And they did, preventing a first down. But had
BYU's offense solved its problems? Though the Cougars then drove 70 yards in just five plays for a tying
touchdown, it was still difficult to say. Most of the
plays were tailor-made to battle a hard-rushing
defense like Missouri's. A delay run by fullback

Casey Tiumalu gained 11 yards. A quick sideline pass to tight end Steve Harper netted 17. A sweep by Tiumalu picked up 18. And the touchdown came from Young's 10-yard quarterback draw.

"That was a beautiful call," said television commentator and former coaching great Bud Wilkinson. "With Missouri's hard rush, it was a good play to run."

Chow had custom-fit this offensive series to Missouri's defensive strength. He deserved at least an assist on the touchdown.

But Mizzou roared right back, taking the ball to the BYU 40 with three first downs. There the drive bogged down and a punt pinned BYU on its own 2-yard line. The Cougars got the ball out to the 19 before Young started feeling Mizzou defensive heat again. He dropped back, saw his protection disintegrate, and scrambled before throwing the ball 15 yards downfield. Receiver Kirk Pendleton went high to catch the ball, but not high enough. Reco Hawkins caught it instead and returned it to BYU's 29-yard line. The Y's offense was moribund, and was quickly killing off the defense, too.

The last time it had benefited from this kind of Cougar generosity, Missouri quickly moved in for a touchdown. But a big stop on Adler on third-and-one by nose guard Brad Smith kept the damage to a field goal. It was 10-7 Mizzou with 3:43 remaining in the half.

The beleaguered BYU defenders were on the field again one minute later to stop a drive starting at midfield. Missouri moved to the 29, when a crushing Kyle Morrell hit jarred a just-caught pass loose from tight end Greg Krahl. Linebacker Todd Shell collected the ball out of the air and ended what could have been a fatal Mizzou drive. Shell received credit for the interception, but "it was all Kyle's doing," he says.

Wilkinson commented on his ESPN telecast that Missouri was stronger man-for-man, but BYU had more finesse. The tough, hard-hitting first half, then, was the Tigers' type of game, and they led 10-7.

The BYU players were not discouraged as they pondered their plight in the halftime locker room. They had played terribly on offense, yet still had ten more total yards than the Tigers. Missouri had controlled the ball 63 percent of the half, but it hadn't pushed the defense around. Steve Young had suffered through his worst passing half of the year, yet still found his team virtually even.

And then there was the well-known tendency of Missouri's offense to fold up and self-destruct in the second half. About 70 percent of Mizzou's 1983 points were scored in the first two quarters. And in close games (ten-point difference or less at the half) the Tigers averaged less than five points a game in the second half.

Surely the nation's most unstoppable offense wouldn't be stopped all game, would it?

Getting stopped wasn't BYU's biggest problem. Steve Harper caught a Steve Young pass early in the third quarter and ran with it to near the 50-yard line. He was hit by Jeff Smith and bobbled the ball. Tracey Mack, a linebacker now but Mizzou's leading rusher the previous year, stole and carried it to the BYU 43.

That was BYU's biggest problem. It was turnover number four, and the Cougar defense was again called on to cover up an offensive mistake. That defense, Missouri was sure, would crack anytime now.

Mizzou took the ball and methodically drove it inside the BYU 10-yard line with powerful runs of four or five yards. The Cougars seemed headed for a certain 10-point deficit midway through the third quarter. But then Missouri's self-destruct button flashed red. Quarterback Marlon Adler, tackled after completing a 12-yard run to BYU's 8, had to be helped off the field with an ankle injury. He wouldn't return.

His replacement was Warren Seitz, a highly regarded 6-foot-4 sophomore. Seitz quickly led the team to the 3 on the first two plays. On third down, he pitched the ball to freshman tailback Jon Redd, who ran it to the 2 before being hit by defensive back Blake Jensen. Jensen's helmet popped the ball free and a gaggle of players converged on it. BYU's Jon Young emerged from the pile-up with the ball. The Cougars had been saved by Missouri's blinking red light.

A rejuvenated Cougar offense, aided by 58 yards in Mizzou penalties, drove the ball to the Tiger 14-yard line. A sack by Taft Sales forced BYU to try a 39-yard field goal. Kicker Lee Johnson missed it to the left.

Just three plays later, BYU tackle Jim Herrman again stripped the ball from Redd. Initially, it seemed that Missouri had recovered the fumble, though Kyle Morrell's jubilant gallop off the field indicated otherwise. When everything had been sorted out, linebacker David Neff, and BYU, had possession. And the little red light began to flare again.

Young dropped the ball over the middle to halfback Eddie Stinnett on the next play, but it was obvious this would gain more than the typical short pass. Stinnett was all by himself in the Mizzou secondary! A block by Kirk Pendleton allowed Stinnett to break to the left and run, solo, into the end zone. He held the ball aloft the final seven yards of his shocking journey. It was so easy that no one even noticed that defensive tackle Dick Chapura had missed blocking the pass at the line of scrimmage by about a foot. Cougar guard Craig Garrick managed to shove Chapura out of the way just before Young's low-flying pass zipped by.

The Cougars' scoring drives had accounted for just 78 seconds of the game's 42 minutes, 21 seconds. But they still had a lead, their first, at 14-10.

The teams traded possessions to end the third quarter. A quick explosion and BYU had taken the lead, but Missouri's low, long rumbling was about to turn the game around again. Seitz and Eric Drain teamed to lead the Tigers on a nine-play, 80-yard drive to open the fourth quarter. All lights were green again, and Mizzou had a 17-14 lead with 10:49 left in the game.

When Adam Haysbert beautifully caught a 16-yard pass at midfield less than two minutes later, it looked like the Cougars were preparing to grab the lead right back. But Casey Tiumalu, after crashing into his own man, helplessly watched as the ball flew out of his hand and Mizzou's Sales pounced on it.

The Tigers were just 47 yards away from taking a 24-14 lead, one that would require another miracle to overcome.

A frustrated Steve Young trotted off the field. The offense had finally begun to click, and now this. He spotted defensive captain Todd Shell and called to him, "Please, just give us one more chance."

But that was asking a lot. BYU's defensive squad would finish only after 37 long minutes of grinding, punishing football. They had struggled to keep up physically with Missouri. They had been forced to come up with big plays repeatedly. The team was, simply put, spent.

Mizzou knew it, too. They pounded at the middle of the Cougar defense for five, two, nine, four, four and seven yards. Everything was hammered between the tackles, just enough to wear BYU defenders down even more, eat up the clock and drive the ball to the 16-yard line. Young nervously paced the sidelines. Mizzou had four more downs. That would be about two more minutes off the clock. He'd end up with less than four minutes to move the team for a winning touchdown. And what if Missouri drove for another first down . . . or touchdown? He didn't even want to think about that. It had to happen right here.

Blitzing Rob Salazar and Marv Allen caught Seitz for a one-yard loss on first down. Then Seitz flipped a wobbly pass to tight end Greg Krahl, who stumbled to the 10. Third and four.

LaVell Edwards gazed forward, hands on knees, nervously chewing gum in machine-gun motion. The crowd, sensing the importance of the next two plays, began to raise the volume. Seitz handed the ball to Santio Barbosa, who surged well into the BYU line to about the 7, where he was met squarely by Salazar, Morrell and Kyle Whittingham.

It was short of a first down, well over a yard short. But Mizzou was going for it. They couldn't fail. Two of three BYU defensive line starters were out with injuries. They'd run at one of the replacements, Larry Hamilton, who'd be blocked out of the way by Conrad Goode — *all-America* Conrad Goode. The power runner, Drain, who had already amassed 115 yards in the game, would take a simple handoff from Seitz. Easy first down. Four more plays to score a touchdown. A 10-point lead. Less than two minutes left.

Dick Felt figured that would be Missouri's plan. He called a 5-3 defense from the press box, a good short-yardage formation. Todd Shell called the defense in the huddle, then added: "Let's show what we're made of. This is the game right here." Morrell took his place, at middle linebacker on the "weak" side in this defense. The last time BYU had used the 5-3, Mizzou had run right at him. He guessed it'd happen again.

The ball was snapped and Seitz handed it to Drain, who looked for a hole near Goode. But Hamilton, the substitute, had stood up the All-American and pushed him backwards. Morrell's correct guess landed him in the hole Drain wanted to run through. He and Hamilton, soon joined by linebackers Marv Allen and Shell, stopped Drain not far past the line of scrimmage.

But Shell was angry when officials marked the ball. He claimed Drain had been stopped further back. The placement would make a measurement necessary. It would obviously be very close. While Shell contended with the referee, he saw Drain trying to move the ball forward even more. The Mizzou running back had made about two feet of progress when he was caught and the ball moved back. The chains were brought to the center of the field, while both teams celebrated their assumed success to each other and the crowd. The chains were stretched, and Shell watched, then leaped, fist thrust into the air, when the end of the chain was placed a foot past the ball. BYU's defense had held under improbable circumstances. And red lights were blinking all over the state of Missouri.

Shell and his colleagues had given Steve Young the chance he asked for. Almost four minutes remained. A breeze of excitement circulated among the 51,000-plus people in Jack Murphy Stadium. They braced themselves for still another exciting Holiday Bowl conclusion.

Young dropped back and hit wide-open receiver Mike Eddo at the 24. The 17-yard gain was a big one, for the Cougars were now well away from their own goal. But Bobby Bell sacked Young for the third time on the next play, streaking in from Young's blind side. Young somehow kept from fumbling, and the ball was on the 11 now, second and 23. In one minute, BYU had gained but four yards.

Young retreated near his goal line and again had to dodge Bell, who once more reached for his jersey. Young darted toward the left sideline and looked downfield. He couldn't believe what he saw. Eddo was running by himself more than 40 yards downfield! The crowd saw the same thing and rose to its feet, almost in unison. Young, the defense rapidly converging on him, planted himself, leaned way back and threw the ball. Eddo waited and waited. "I could see three defenders running toward me as fast as they could," he says. "I just wanted to catch the ball and hold on. I thought it'd never get to me."

It did get there, and Eddo did catch the ball launched 54 yards by Young. The fast-closing defenders downed Eddo at the Mizzou 36-yard line. Young didn't see the completion. He was flattened by Robert Curry just after letting go, but the crowd told him the ball had made it.

Warren Powers, now nervously pacing the sidelines, signaled to his players to calm down. He was obviously talking to himself as well.

Two more quick completions gave the Cougars

another first down at the 25. A delay to Tiumalu lost two yards, and BYU called time out. Only 1:26 remained. Young then managed to release a pass to Tiumalu, standing near the sideline, just as he was hit. The BYU fullback powered his way to the 16, dragging defenders along the last several yards. Third and one, 50 seconds left.

Young didn't see Mizzou's Jeff Smith blitzing him. Smith leveled the quarterback and the ball flew loose. Replays on television later showed that Young had started a passing motion, but it was ruled a fumble anyway. A wild scramble began. Missouri's Curry had the ball in reach but dived too far for it. Sales was about to cover it when BYU's Garrick slid past and grabbed it. Sales kicked at the ground like a child in a tantrum. Both he and a teammate had come so close to recovering the ball, yet BYU maintained a fortunate possession.

A fourth and 10 still had to be converted. Only 37 seconds remained. Young approached the line and quieted the crowd. He flashed seven fingers to each side, then took the snap. Receivers were well-covered downfield, so he tossed the ball to Waymon Hamilton flaring out of the backfield. The ball was a little behind him, but Hamilton managed to catch it and sprint for the first down marker. He got there just as Jerome Caver did, whose hit drove him out of bounds one yard past the first-down stake.

First and 10 on the 14. Norm Chow, from the press box, called "fake ride 28 QB screen left," which, translated, is a handoff to the tailback, who starts to sweep right but then throws the ball back to the quarterback, who runs with it from there. A gimmick play. Running back coach Lance Reynolds, seated next to Chow, "looked at me [Chow] like I was nuts."

But there was something to Chow's madness. In Missouri's man-to-man defense, Young would not be covered. With his athletic ability, he could do the most damage to this defense by *running* the ball. An earlier quarterback draw had worked well, and Chow thought this might, too. There was time left, anyway, and if the play didn't work, they'd still have at least three more chances to score.

Fake ride 28 QB screen left. The play was practiced whenever BYU went over its gimmick plays — typically two or three times a week. But the players rarely took the complex play seriously when running through it. "Make sure you tell me before you call *that* one," Edwards told Chow once while watching the play being rehearsed.

But there was not time for permission now. The play was relayed to quarterback coach Mike Holmgren on the sidelines, who passed it on to the BYU offensive huddle.

Mike Eddo, who stood next to Holmgren and Edwards, asked which play was about to be run. When told, he exclaimed "Ohmygosh," and leaned far forward to watch. It would be an adventure for everyone.

"I loved it," said Young of the call. "I thought it was a gutsy decision. It's one of those plays you just have to wait and see develop."

Eddie Stinnett took Young's handoff and began to run to the right. Then he stopped. His off-balance pass easily cleared the two players pursuing him.

But there was one little problem. Mizzou's Bobby Bell, who had wreaked havoc in BYU's backfield all evening, stood between Stinnett's pass and Young,

Steve Young was befuddled by the Mizzou defense most of the game, but found the end zone (facing page) when it counted most.

wondering what on earth was happening. It dawned on him when he saw the ball arching high toward the quarterback. He had a choice. He could easily tackle Young after he caught the pass, or try to tip or intercept the ball. He chose the latter.

He jumped, then with dismay saw the pass clear his fingertips by inches. Young recovered quickly and caught the "second half" of the ball, then

headed for the end zone. He wove past stunned defenders and ran untouched until hit by Reco Hawkins at the goal line. Falling over the line, he jumped up and high-stepped around the end zone, holding the ball high in the air by that same "second half."

The stadium was in a frenzy. BYU players mobbed Young in the end zone, and each other on the sidelines. The 51,480 in the stadium, mostly BYU supporters, looked like a wave from the field as they jumped up and down in loud exultation. TV and radio announcers yelled the unbelievable details to disbelieving viewers and listeners. Powers stormed up and down his side of the field, arms flailing.

But wait. The Missouri coach stopped abruptly. A penalty flag had been dropped on the play. He stood, hands on hips, daring the official to allow the touchdown. The signal: dead ball foul. The touchdown would stand! Powers jerked as if drawing pistols and shooting the referee, then turned and stalked away. BYU's enthusiastic celebration of the touchdown had drawn an unsportsmanlike conduct penalty. But it was still 21-17 BYU, and only 23 seconds remained.

Seitz tried three desperation passes in the waning moments. The first two fell incomplete inside a circling wall of BYU defenders. The third was intercepted by Morrell, who ran with the ball high above his head well into the Missouri sideline, as if to say, "Does *this* show you?"

Warren Powers had been "showed." "It was a hard-fought game, and our guys played very well," he said in gracious post-game comments. "BYU is an excellent team and deserved to win. I want to say that I think Steve Young is the best quarterback I've ever seen in college football."

But the spirit of William Duncan Vandiver wasn't

so easily quelled in Mizzou's locker room, revealed Provo's *Daily Herald.* Drain, whose *"What* is it?" comment on the Holiday Bowl typified his team's view of the whole affair, said: "If BYU is number 9, we should be right up there with them. BYU is a pretty good team compared to those we've played against in the Big 8 this year . . . but I wasn't at all impressed with them. We should have scored every time we had the ball because their defensive line wasn't that strong."

And Bobby Bell, in a classic reversal of roles, offered: "BYU didn't give us the respect we deserve. We still probably won't get it from them." But manifesting sudden respect for the team that had just defeated him, he said, "BYU is right up there with [4-6-1] Kansas University. BYU didn't beat us in the fourth quarter. We beat ourselves, and that's what we have to live with."

Concerning his erroneous decision to jump for the Stinnett pass rather than pursue Young, Bell speculated to the Kansas City *Times* that his father, the ex-NFL great, "probably won't let me back in the house."

Gee, Bobby, how could he, especially when goofing against a team like BYU?

The Cougars obviously hadn't showed Tiger players, who were, to their minds, now 12-0 and counting.

Norm Chow didn't see LaVell Edwards until the team was aboard the bus after the game. He apologized, tongue-in-cheek, for not running fake ride 28 QB screen left past the head coach first. No apology necessary, he was told.

Steve Young, who had completed 10 of 11 passes for 145 yards in the crucial fourth quarter, became the *second* BYU quarterback to lead his team to a bowl victory. It was a storybook ending to his collegiate career, and a perfect bridge to a lucrative contract with the United States Football League's Los Angeles Express.

It was time for Missouri Attorney General John Ashcroft to pay up. He had made a little wager with his counterpart from Utah, David Wilkinson, over the outcome of the Holiday Bowl: the loser would sing the other team's fight song on the steps of his capitol building. Ashcroft, complete with band accompaniment, launched into "Rise and Shout."

The attorney general used as a footstool a stuffed cougar, bedecked in a Missouri hat and tagged with a sign that read: "When I grow up, I want to be a Tiger."

You never can show some people.